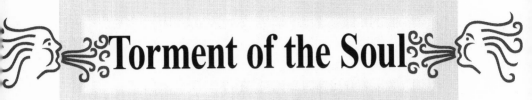

Torment of the Soul

Suicidal Depression and Spirituality

Benedict Auer, O.S.B. and Jessy A. Ang, M.D.

authorHOUSE®

AuthorHouse™
1663 Liberty Drive, Suite 200
Bloomington, IN 47403
www.authorhouse.com
Phone: 1-800-839-8640

First published by AuthorHouse 10/25/2007

ISBN: 978-1-4343-2180-0 (sc)
ISBN: 978-1-4343-2181-7 (hc)

Library of Congress Control Number: 2007904942

Printed in the United States of America
Bloomington, Indiana

This book is printed on acid-free paper.

For all who suffer from depression
whether they continue to suffer with their illness
or have ended their lives,
and for their families, friends and therapists
who try to understand their pain and anguish.

Contents

Acknowledgements

I can never thank Dr. Jessy Ang enough. He inspired this book on the very first session I had with him concerning my bipolar disorder. He planted the seed, I watered it, and as St. Paul says God made it grow. His dedication as a Christian psychiatrist has greatly inspired me and shown me the compassion and care needed to be a healer of men and women.

My community at St. Martin's Abbey gave me the opportunity to be a Visiting Scholar at Weston Jesuit School of Theology in Cambridge, MA and access to their library and the libraries of Harvard University. It was a wonderful opportunity that combined my twenty-fifth anniversary as a priest and a mini-sabbatical that produced this book. Abbot Neal Roth, O.S.B. who through his understanding and at times mystification helped me understand myself and led me in directions I would never have chosen except through his direction as Abbot.

I would like to thank my first reader, Johanna Mitchell, who gently but firmly showed me the errors of my ways and made this book understandable and readable. And then my last reader, Betsy Astolfi, who was able to make suggestions that after so many readings still needed to be made. There are so many people I should thank and am afraid I will leave out, but I need to thank those who have remained supportive through good times and bad. Working with a manic-depressive person is no easy task and so I thank Susan Leyster who has worked with me for almost twenty years, Nick Kucharik, Brother Luke Devine, O.S.B. and those who have remained friends through the darkness of my illness. And naturally my family who have remained supportive through it all: my brother, David, and his wife, Alice, and their three children and spouses, and their seven grandchildren and my sister, Mary. Finally, I must thank my late mother, Marcelline, and my dad, William, for living with my illness even when we did not know I had it.

INTRODUCTION

In 1961, the famed Swedish director Ingmar Bergman created a tightly constructed and very realistic film about the hunger and loneliness of the human soul called "Through a Glass Darkly." The phrase is from St. Paul. It is an attempt by the apostle to capture in words a theology that works from the viewpoint that God is hidden and remains so. This viewpoint often uses the scriptural statement "see the face of God and die." In Bergman's film, the entire story takes place on an island during a span of twenty-four hours. The film is an interchange of the young woman who is married to one of the men on the island, the daughter of another, and the sister of a third man. The female protagonist meanders through the film losing her mind. In the last scene, the father and son exchange thoughts about God, but for all its solemn simplicity, it rings hollow. The end result is that the viewer leaves the film psychologically desensitized. This book will seem like a Swedish film at times. If not careful, our talk about God will seem hollow and echo off the recesses of our minds -- a Simon and Garfunkel song that plays over and over, but gives no answers, only questions.

When we step into the world of depression, we find ourselves walking through a glass darkly into a world where everything is "Fun House" distorted. It is the house of mirrors at a local amusement park that distorts you into a thousand different shapes that you cannot find the real you. The reader will want simple answers. There are none. Hopefully by the end of this book, we will not leave you with only a hollow conversation about God and nothing that will change lives.

What we will look at in this book is spirituality both as found in mainstream religion and also in alternative spiritualities, and its impact on depressed individuals who attempt suicide and their associated communities. This book will also look at the benefit of spirituality for dealing with despair, and also see what tools there are for the counselor and eventually the family to cope with the various stages of depression before or after an attempt that is unsuccessful or after a person has taken his or her life.

James Joyce wrote a short story called *The Dead*. In this story, the characters are paralyzed by life and caught in a living limbo.

They cannot see themselves and walk zombie-like through life.

When we attempt to understand the life of another, we are always at a loss. We can never know why the great St. Teresa of Avila, a spiritual genius, suffered, if she really did, from anorexia and other mental disorders. Or why St. John of the Cross called his experiences of depression and abandonment by God, "the Dark Night of the Soul." But even though we stumble, we need to ask these questions to gain insight into the illness called depression, the black abyss that many people fall into and cannot escape. It is during this state of torment that many people attempt or succeed in taking their lives. Those people today are often said to have died "from the illness of depression" and not from suicide. It may seem like a play on words but it is not. Depression is an illness. Some illnesses such as cancer or heart disease, eventually kill unless properly treated. Depression does the same.

The question arises: Is medication and therapy the only way to treat depression, or is there something else that might help a person battle the torment that comes from depression? We are faced with the problem that historians have faced in analyzing the dead. If a suicide is successful, the story has ended for that person and all we have are the survivors: family, friends and therapists. But not all suicides are successful; many people think about killing themselves or even attempt to do so, but survive. Why do some people think about it and not act upon it?

This study will start with the cultural origins of suicide. When did utter despair with life first cause people to take their own lives? We will look at the Asian as well as the European beginnings of this phenomenon. The reasons that are given are numerous, but there is a pattern. Although more time will be spent with the European cultural aspects of suicide because of the influence on American civilization, the sociological and cultural aspects of suicide in many societies will be discussed, for suicide is cross-cultural.

In the second chapter, the biological aspects of depression and suicide will be investigated. If depression is caused by a chemical imbalance, is medication then the only solution? Why are some people in a family affected by depression and others not? This chapter will look at what scientists know about the mind and how it works. Only in the 19th century did science really attempt to learn about the mind. In recent years, more and more has been learned, but we still are neophytes in the search to understand the mind and the many illnesses connected to its mechanisms and machinations. Only if we try to understand the mind that produces depression can we address what can be done about it.

In Chapter three, spirituality will be defined with the attitudes and teachings of religion on suicide. Judaism, Christianity (Catholicism), Muslim, Buddhism, Hinduism, and other religions will be explored. Do these teachings stop people from committing suicide or does religion or even spirituality make a difference at all? In the coverage of religion in this chapter, the historical approach will be followed going from the ancient world to the present. A major question will be: How has the stance of the various beliefs changed over the years? More importantly, what do the various spiritual paths now teach or at least tacitly accept or approve? This will tie up the cultural origins of suicide, the biological implications of depression, and finally the spiritual path that is a component for some on the journey from depression into wellness. Or if suicide is chosen, why and how could spirituality have had an impact on the depressed person?

After forming this triangle of information, we will use case studies to fathom out some possible characteristics of suicidal thought, and when spirituality has been a success by giving hope and when it has not. A number of famous people will be used; Vincent Van Gogh, Abraham Lincoln, Anne Sexton, and a few saints such as Teresa of Avila and John of the Cross that provided religious vocabulary for depression that is used to the present day. After the famous, we will use present-day case studies from our own experiences with the permission of the persons involved.

We will try to tie the triangle of how suicide came about, how depression affects a person who has the illness, and how spirituality impacts depressed people who try to end their lives or think about suicide. In conclusion, the major question is whether spirituality makes a difference. The conclusion deals with the configuration of the above three pronged triad and whether somehow spirituality gives meaning to one's life. This is not a scientific or sociological study. Rather this book is for the common layperson or therapist who needs help in understanding the ramifications of a suicidal family member, friend or patient.

An extensive bibliography will follow the conclusion for those who wish to explore this topic further. But be warned, there is little on this topic in America, but there are numerous papers and articles from Britain, Australia and New Zealand. American therapists and psychiatrists seem reluctant to include spirituality in their practices, but in the other three countries mentioned, they seem fearless.

This book is an act of love. Dr. Jessy Ang is a psychiatrist with an extensive practice of patients suffering from depression and has a great interest in bipolar disorder. I am one of his patients. During my diagnostic interview, Dr. Ang mentioned that he was interested in this topic of spirituality and depression/suicide. He planted a seed that took over two years to grow. Sadly it was a suicide that triggered or maybe provoked the writing of this book. I performed a wedding and the bride's brother, who had been institutionalized three times for manic-depression, was able to come but was highly sedated. The brother even took part in the ceremony. Afterward I spoke with him and saw the pain he was in. He seemed to be a very "spiritual" person, although unchurched, who had lost all hope in his life. A week after the wedding, he jumped off a bridge into a river and died. As his parents said, "He died from the illness of depression." The question that Dr. Ang had originally asked "What role does spirituality play in the treatment and struggle against suicide?" struck home. That question has produced this book.

We will look at spirituality both as found in mainstream religion and also in alternative spiritualities, and its impact on depressed individuals who attempt suicide and their associated communities. This book will also look at the benefit of spirituality for dealing with despair. It will also explore what tools there are for the counselor and eventually the family to cope with the various stages of depression before or after an attempt that is unsuccessful or after a person has taken his/her life. Hopefully if one person is able to read this book and come away with some ideas that will help them understand or be more compassionate, this book will have been a success.

Chapter One:
A Cultural History of Depression and Suicide

From the beginning of time, at least written time, there seems to be mention of a condition, no matter what it is called, of "darkness" or "torment" or eventually "melancholia." The terminology may differ but the explanation describes a mood that is essentially black and causes one to think of killing oneself. The words change over the years, but the experience or feeling does not. Life loses its meaning. One falls deeper into an emotional abyss that seems to be endless and impossible to climb out of. The feelings of darkness are sometimes preceded or followed by great feelings of elation or productivity, splurges of creativity and excitement over the littlest things. The records we have of these emotional experiences come from artists, poets, writers, and educated people who had the talent and also the ability to write down their experiences for future generations to read and muse over.

Today, we have different terminology to describe the experiences of these far off ancestors who tried to tell us what they were going through and often did not have the words to write about the emptiness they felt, the abandonment they experienced, or the temptation to end their earthly existence. These feelings are certainly not new. Maybe we talk about the illness more now and it has become somewhat more socially acceptable to tell people what a person is experiencing and how they feel. We have created words that capture experiences. But still these words limp; even though they do express some of the pain a person feels who is attacked by these moods. And there are people, professionals such as psychiatrists and therapists, who can try to help the person fallen by such illness. But how did we get from there to here? It is a complex story, but worth telling.

Depression and its sometime accompanying companion, suicide have been with us as long as there has been "recorded" expressions of feelings. In previous centuries, the word depression was not used to indicate a pathological set of symptoms. The earlier period of history spoke of *melancholia*. The ancient Greeks recognized depression as a medical condition, but did not distinguish it from other mental illnesses. This attitude persisted through to the nineteenth century.

The word "suicide," or literally self-murder, has its origins in the Latin word *Suicidium*, which is composed of *sui*, the genitive of *suus*, meaning his or self, and the term, *cidium*, deriving from the verb *caedere* which means to kill, chop or stab. In other words, "to kill oneself" would be the closest translation. Nils Retterstol, in an article in the Norwegian Journal of Suicidology, writes that suicide "seems to be a relatively new term, dating perhaps from the 1500's."

For the purpose of this chapter, we will look at suicide from two different viewpoints:

1. Social and institutionalized suicide
2. Individual and personal suicide

It is the second viewpoint that will be the center of our attention. The first form of suicide can be simply defined as a self-destruction demanded by the society of an individual. For instance, in India a widow is still, even though it has been legally done away with, expected in many cases to throw herself on her husband's funeral pyre as it is burning thus killing herself. In ancient Egypt, slaves who built the pyramids were expected to remain in the tomb with the master until they too died. Now, whether this was voluntary or not has been debated by archaeologists. Slaves were often drugged as their remains show us or killed before the tomb was sealed and that certainly cannot be called voluntary suicide. In primitive Alaska, the natives when ill or sick would be left behind to die. This was a voluntary act and can be considered a form of societal suicide. In nomadic societies, the old and sick were a liability to the tribe and therefore they were either left behind or would sacrifice themselves for the good of the tribe.

Assisted suicide might fall under this social suicide, when the elderly person or sick person may consider themselves a burden to his/her family. Financially, the burden for an elderly person is prohibitive to many families. Children may be forced to take care of ailing or elderly parents which may cost the children their home or life savings. With their quality of life near zero and their knowledge of the burden they are causing their children, some elderly people may socially consider it the right thing to do – kill themselves for the good of their families. However, the social dimensions of these suicides are more important than the personal innuendoes. The person feels that society is unable to support them in their dying circumstances. Thus they choose death because they cannot face life. It is their burden on their families or society that forces them into committing suicide.

In addition, institutionalized or social suicide may involve patriotic disgrace. In Japanese society, with the ending of World War II some Japanese felt disgraced and the only option was an honorable death that was self-inflicted. Kamikazes also were only able to complete their missions by flying their planes into enemy ships. Those that did so died honorably because their suicides served their society. They sacrificed themselves for the motherland, and for their emperor who had commanded them to do this act. Finally, agents for governments sent off to spy or do other covert service also may be given no options except to kill themselves if they are caught by the enemy government or its agents rather than possibly betray their country.

All of these suicides are social or institutionalized forms of self-destruction. The individual may make a choice but the pressure from society and other social institutions, such as family or tribe, force a decision on the person that makes the act no longer personal, but demanded by the society in which they live. The pressure is greater than the person can resist and therefore their psychological stamina is destroyed or their free will is mitigated if not taken completely away.

Personal or individual suicides can be characterized differently.

Honor may play a part in the suicide or feelings of failure, but frequently depression or some form of mental illness plays a part in these suicides. One could almost say that all suicides on a personal or individual level are caused by some failure or conceived failure on the part of the person who is killing himself/herself. Once backed against a wall, it is very hard mentally to find a way out. Everything, and possibly everyone, has failed to respond to the person's situation. There is no recourse except to end one's existence. One could argue that at this stage of a person's life that a form of depression or *melancholia* sets in so that the person sees no other way out of the situation. A person loses their job, their house and car, and finally their family. One is an absolute failure in his/her own eyes. There is no way out and no help in sight. It is then that the person feels that only death will solve this horrible situation. Usually the person has a myopic view of the reality of their situation and feels lost and abandoned. Sometimes an individual cannot see beyond themselves.

This chapter will concentrate or try to focus on only the suicide caused by depression. But in order to understand this type of suicide, it is necessary to look at the history of suicide or at least the norms that different societies have concerning suicide. A short survey of the historical ramifications of suicide may help put into perspective the act and its approval or disapproval in secular terms. For instance, in ancient Greece suicide was considered a totally disgraceful act. Life was a gift from the gods, and to take it was an effrontery to the gods who gave life to a person. If one killed oneself, a person was not allowed the burial rites that were the right of a common citizen. Interestingly enough, Pythagoras, the mathematician, had worked out a formula proving that suicide might topple the balance of souls that he had mathematically worked out for the earth. He had created a formula that actually calculated how many finite souls there could be on the earth at a given time. A suicide could topple the pyramid of life by creating a vacuum that might destroy the entire human population. Therefore suicide was an act against humanity and a great social injustice. It had to be expressly forbidden.

Plato thought suicide was a wrong and improper act. His argument was even more bizarre. Plato said that all humans were made by the gods and were the gods' soldiers. If a person killed himself or herself the act was not murder, but desertion, making a person a traitor in the eyes of the state. Therefore, no burial would be allowed for such a person. Plato saw some exceptions; such as horrible ailments, terrible poverty or profound grief. Even so, those who died by their own hands were buried outside of the town and their hands were cut off and buried far away from the perpetrator of their self-killing.

Aristotle condemned suicide as well, for it was a sin against the fatherland. And a person who killed himself or herself was considered weak. But the Greek condemnation was no way universal. Exceptions were made. Themistocles who poisoned himself rather than betray the Greeks to the Persian invaders was a hero.

The School of the Stoics developed a slightly different attitude toward suicide. As gradually the belief in the old gods deteriorated, it was still necessary that one condemned suicide. However, the actual school itself started to develop a way to approach suicide as an honorable and appropriate act. The reasons were quite simple and revolved around honor. An additional one was added: when poverty, chronic illness, or mental disease made death more attractive than life. One thing to keep in mind is that the Stoics were duty bound to live for others.

Zeno, the founder of the stoic philosophy, according to Nils Retterstol, had found life enjoyable until he was 98 years old.

Then he fell and dislocated his big toe. This so disturbed his existence that he went home and hanged himself. Death by dislocated toe seems an extreme reason to kill oneself, but that is the myth around the death of Zeno.

Seneca, another Stoic, argued that suicide was a way to end suffering. Even as late as Marcus Aurelius, in the second century, the Emperor wrote that although suicide might be an option to an imperfect life, that it must be performed quietly and with no theatrical gestures.

In Roman law, suicide was considered positively if performed to avoid dishonor, an expression of grief over the loss of someone, or in service of one's country. The ancient world seemed to be open to institutional or social suicide, but found little understanding of depression or the ramifications of depression on an individual. This naturally affected the European attitude toward suicide. While Roman and Greek culture were not that open to suicide, they did allow it under certain circumstances.

It was not until the eighteenth century, when Christianity was being challenged that once again philosophers started to question the responsibility of a person who killed himself/herself. Montesquieu, Voltaire, and Rousseau defended the individual's right to take their own life. In this century, David Hume addressed this seriously when he wrote his essay "On Suicide" in 1783. It could not even be published in his lifetime. He went back to the Greeks and took their viewpoint that certain things made life unbearable, such as extreme poverty or pain. An interesting idea was that man did commit a crime against himself for no man would discard his life while it was still worth living. It was during this century the idea that suicide was not a crime but rather a mental illness developed. J.M. Merian declared this idea before the Berlin Academy, which started the church modifying its views on suicide for people of unsound mind. Wolfgang Goethe in *The Sorrows of Young Werther*, a story that included a young man taking his life, caused an epidemic of suicides throughout Europe much like those in Japan today.

As time went on in the West, many attitudes toward suicide changed. In the 19th century, Arthur Schopenhauer anticipated modern psychiatric perceptions of suicide when he wrote that man did not choose suicide because he did not want life but rather because he was so unhappy with life that death seemed the only option. A Chinese priest recently told me, that while in middle school, he read Schopenhauer and he has been a major influence on his life. But as the century continued, suicide was still a disgrace and often was a family's best kept secret. When I was in graduate school, I studied Emile Durkheim's "La Suicide" (1897). Durkheim's work is probably the most important book written on the topic. His final summation states that the better integrated a person is in his/her society, the better he/she will be protected against destructive acts, such as suicide.

In the twentieth century, World War II cheapened life. Millions of people dying made life seem inconsequential. Eventually two philosophers, Jean-Paul Sartre and Albert Camus formulated what for them seemed a philosophy of suicide that fit the society of the post-war western world. For Sartre, "…suicide is an absurdity which allows my life to succumb to the absurd." For Camus there was only one serious philosophical problem: suicide. For him killing oneself was not the answer, even though meaninglessness, absurdity, alienation permeate life. Life was absurd to the existentialist. Society in the west had reached a conclusion yet it did not differ so much from other societies.

In Asian culture, people were more open to suicide but once again, honor played an important role in the acceptance of suicide as a part of societal structure. Ritual suicide has historically been relatively common in Asian countries, as means of escaping tragedy, shame and as a form of political protest. The moral systems in China did not look favorably on suicide. And as in many Asian cultures suicide has been tied closely with gender today and historically. There are many examples of women committing suicide in pre-modern Chinese history over issues of oppression and misfortune. It still seems to be a problem today since China is the only country where female suicides outnumber male suicides two to one. The difficulty seems to center around husbands and mother-in-laws looking down on wives or when women fell into shame. As in most Asian cultures, if a woman had an affair, suicide was a way to escape shame.

In China, popular stories glamorize suicide. Lovers unable to unite are joined together in death. Examples of this attitude are found in two novels, *A Dream of Red Mansions* and *The Butterfly Lovers*. Death by suicide was one of the only ways for the lovers to be united if opposed by the family.

During the Chinese Cultural Revolution (1966-1976), many public figures supposedly committed suicide, but insiders say they were killed. Lao She, a famous writer, was listed as a suicide during this period. It is rumored the she was murdered by the Communist government.

Today, suicide among females in China is very high. In 2006, it was stated that China now had the highest rate of suicide, surpassing even Japan, according to the sparse information available. It is mainly among the poor, uneducated and rural women that these suicides occur. Because of who and where the suicides are committed, many that would not be fatal in the urban areas are fatal for these country women. But as China becomes more and more urbanized people are committing suicide in large cities due to the stress of modern life and unemployment.

In Japan, attitudes are basically tolerant toward suicides. The recent rash of suicides in Japan have made the Japanese reconsider their views on suicide but that will be discussed later in this chapter when youth suicide and "copycat suicide" are discussed.

In the West, as the Church took over control of suicidal attitudes of all Christians, the Church teaching became the rule by which everything was judged. Philosophers as we have seen started to return to the Greek ideas and thus differed from the Church. In other parts of the world, this may have been true or may not have been true. Religion shaped many cultures, Christianity in the West, Islam in the Middle East, but Buddhism and Hinduism did not have as great a control over the people as did the other two religions. And both Asian religions were less stringent in their dealings with suicides.

In general, there seems to be a pattern that crosses cultures and continents. In most societies, it seems to be acceptable if you kill yourself for honor, your country, or if you reach the end of your rope: poverty, illness, and so forth. Both of these reasons seem to be found from one culture to another, cross-fertilizing the culture. Another aspect of this approach is what is called a suicide culture.

Within a culture, eastern or western, there is a somewhat accepted belief that suicide is contagious; that one suicide may lead, or does lead, to a spate of copycat deaths. In this day and age, there are schools of thought on the idea of a "suicide culture" and whether it is a true phenomenon or a myth. This is an aspect of suicide and its social implications that is presently being studied. The study has had mixed reception in the learned community.

Paul Marsden of the Graduate Research Centre in the Social Sciences, University of Sussex, believes that suicide culture is real and occurs in societies around the world. In his paper "Is Suicide Contagious? A Case Study" in *Applied Memetics* (2001), Marsden claims that "suicide contagion is said to occur when exposure to suicidal acts appears to trigger copycat suicidal acts". One suicide gives birth to many suicides. Suicide is not a solitary act but one which raises questions that lead to many people seeing it as a way out of a life that seems to have no hope.

In some very small towns in Australia, there had been a wave of suicides caused by the impossibility to escape the endless humdrum of monotony that exist in these bush settlements. The lack of avenues of escape create depressive situations that lead to the suicides of young people that observed one person killing themselves as a means of freeing themselves from an unchanging and often imprisoning situation of their existence. These deaths eventually lead to multiple people ending their lives within a few weeks or months. There seems to be a direct correlation between personal depression over a seemingly unchangeable situation and the escapism of suicide. The correlation is not statistically or psychologically proven, but only suggested by the data.

Youth suicide, and it tends to be youth, although it can happen with other age groups, is most prevalent in the rural communities of Australia where life seems to hold no future. While I was a visiting lecturer in Bendigo in Victoria, Australia, I found students depressed over a lack of jobs and a future in that area of the country. While lecturing at a rural branch of a university, a student raised her hand and asked, "Are they keeping us in school because there is no employment nor will there ever be?" And another chimed in, "We have no future. I am being trained as a teacher and there are no jobs for teachers available anywhere." The class seemed depressed as a whole, and a prime candidate for copycat suicide. If the newspapers and television portray the young person who has killed himself/herself as a hero with a misunderstood yet essentially good character, other suicidal youth may imagine they will be eulogized the same way and their errors in life will be forgiven and all will be well after their death.

Thus the media plays a part in the creation and continuation of a suicide culture.

Some years ago, one of my students who was a heavy drug user, was killed in a car accident. The following Sunday I preached on the fact that I had attended his wake and was amazed at how many students stood around the corner to attend the viewing of the body. The next day, the young man's brother confronted me and told me that his brother had reformed and that his death was not a death of self-destruction. Yet many of the students saw it as a suicide. They looked at him and his death as a glorification of the drug culture and he was a hero, to be emulated and not someone who had failed in life. His apparent suicide was a step taken that freed him from his trials and struggle with drugs. It was a good act.

The media, of course, can't be blamed for the suicide culture, anymore than the suicidal youth can. Neither exists in a vacuum. But the glorification of suicide as a way out from boredom and a lack of opportunity can create an ambiance that is primed for group suicide.

On the other hand, some scholars believe that a suicide culture is a myth. Mark Moran, writer of the article "Is suicide contagious- or preventative?" says that exposure to suicide may actually prevent copycat behavior. A study in *The American Journal of Epidemiology* (June 15, 2001) revealed that 153 "suicide attempters" in Harris County, Texas, were "exposed" to suicide, whereas there were 513 suicide attempts in those who were not exposed to the suicide of friends, family and media icons. Basically, people were less inclined to commit suicide if they had known someone who had died by their own hand. In Moran's article, James Mercy, MD, goes so far as to state that exposure to suicide may actually be beneficial to those living in the society; that if you're not close to the dead person, and they have died recently, the death will prove the inappropriateness and incomprehensibility of suicide and prevent another death. This exposure to suicide may be an experience that leads to the question "Why?" and the answers come back with responses such as "There is no reason." or "This was stupid on his/her part."

Another use of the term "suicide culture" comes from Japanese society. For Japanese youth to get into a good college or high school, they must study hard because failure to get into a good school is considered shameful for the student, their family and their teachers. Businessmen are also under a great deal of pressure to succeed in their careers. According to Chika Watanabe of the American School in Japan, "…for the Japanese, suicide is not the same as giving up. It is a dignified resignation, a form of compensation to spare the shame of oneself or of others". Thus suicide has become a part of popular and traditional culture in Japan. In 2006, through Internet exposure, young people are able to communicate with each other and find mutual thinking peers who are afraid of killing themselves alone. They find companionship which leads to a strength that solitude does not allow. Some youths band together and one of them having a car meets with the others at a designated location. Then the group seals the windows of the automobile with tape and they light a small charcoal burner. All three or four people enter the car and die from asphyxiation. Another example is two young Japanese men who met on the Internet and arranged to meet at a cliff in a remote area of Japan. They planned to jump together off the cliff into the ravine below. One jumped but the other changed his mind and did not complete the act, leaving the newspapers the opportunity to inform Japanese youth that they cannot trust each other. And finally, in Japan it is quite common for unrequited lovers to meet by the base of beautiful Mount Fuji and kill themselves to show the world their unrequited love or get even with their parents. All these show a societal approach to suicide; yet each stems from a depression that tells them that nothing will get better, only worse, so suicide is a way out. Suicide coupled with social pressure creates a depression that envisions relief from a life that shows no hope. Meaning in life is lost because it is based on events or things that are unattainable. Without meaning, life is not worth living so death is the only answer.

Suicide can be made glamorous by media coverage or Internet explanation/advice of how to kill oneself. The glamour for young people is found in the fact that others are doing the act, and being covered by the news media, which leads to the idea of "why can't I do the same." It may call attention to their personal situation, such as being unemployed, inability to gain admission to a university, or a failed love affair. Japan has the highest rate of suicide in the world, followed by China who is rapidly surpassing its Asian neighbor and followed by the Scandinavian countries. The latter possibly triggered by the winters, the seeming endless grayness of days that leads to sun deprivation. This is frequently called SAD. SAD is an acronym for "Seasonal Affective Disorder" more commonly known as the "Winter Blues." This disorder occurs primarily in winter months with a higher incidence in the northern latitudes, such as Scandinavia. During extended cloudy summer weather, many people throughout the world report SAD symptoms as well. This illness adds to the cultural and societal influences on a depressed person. Any cultural history of suicide must include any such factors many of which were unknown just a few years back and therefore unshared. This fact may be just another aspect of the entire picture that one should consider in trying to understand a suicide.

Historically, these authors find the social and cultural history of suicide to be muddled. There is no one-way to look at the development of attitudes toward suicidal depression. The Greek philosophers mention it almost indirectly. Western culture stresses that honor is a reason for suicide as does Asian culture. But all of these cultures have exceptions. The openness of some cultures in understanding suicide through man's history such as the Asian culture speaks to us in today's world. The narrow Western interpretation of how suicide is understood, and even what should be done about those who die by their own hands, starts with the Greeks, especially the philosophers. Different cultures have come into the 21st century, layered with social, cultural and psychological attitudes. But before we go into the religious attitudes that must be superimposed on this cultural history, it is probably time to look at the biological and psychological approaches and attitudes toward suicidal depression and see what we know and how little we are really able to understand.

Chapter Two:
The Causal Background of
Depression and Suicide

There is no single reason that can explain why a person is depressed. Depression has multiple causes that either separately or together make a person depressed. A psychiatrist or psychologist cannot say, "This is the reason you are depressed," or "Absolutely, I can trace your depression to this episode in your life." Depression does not work that way. Sadly, the illness is much more complex than that. As one professional wrote," Unlike the flu, which is caused by a virus, depression can be caused by many factors."

In this chapter, we are going to cover "clinical depression", also referred to as "major depression" or just "depression." This is defined as "a mood disorder that may occur only once in a person's lifetime, or in clusters of episodes that typically last 9-16 months." People who suffer from depression may also suffer manic episodes and be diagnosed as manic-depressive or with bipolar disorder. Individuals who suffer from major depression or bipolar disorder have a high rate of suicide or attempted suicide as part of their illness. It is our purpose to look closely at the relationship between the two issues, depression and suicide. I will now share my own experience about the battle with depression and suicide and an analysis of this battle.

When I joined a religious community at the age of thirty-six, I did not know I suffered from manic-depression and neither did my community. Since the age of fourteen, I had suffered from bouts of highs and lows, but just considered them part of my life, a cross I had to bear. I had a successful career as a high school teacher. The schools where I instructed, just thought I was an enthusiastic teacher with creative ideas who used the summers as a time to regenerate and overcome my black moods of depression. Luckily, the summer vacations were sufficient when I was in my twenties and thirties to rejuvenate and return in the fall the "outstanding" teacher who had taught the academic year before.

At the age of thirty-six when I felt called to the religious life, I felt it was only a new and more sanctified approach to what I had been doing up to that point. All my teaching had been in Catholic schools. I had attended Mass most of my life on a daily basis. I had tried studying before for the priesthood in the minor seminary, but had left. I had matured by my thirties or so I thought, and now was the time to fulfill my dream of becoming a monk and a priest. I took all the tests, although at that time they were not as many as today, talked to the Vocation Director, and appeared to be suited for the rigors of the religious and monastic life.

In the year of my entrance into the community, I was the only novice. Yet the community still had in place all the rules and work that they did when there were seven novices. The challenge was formidable. I was thirty-six and alone in a novitiate designed in the 1940's or earlier. The rule was still blind obedience. You did it because you were told. Seemingly on the surface it would appear it would not work for a manic-depressive. But for a bipolar person, structure is life saving, literally. As one of my psychiatrists later told me, "Monasticism saved your life. You should be dead from either suicide or alcoholism." My community at the time knew none of this.

I had a few minor breakdowns during my novitiate but no more than I had had over the rest of the years of my life. At fourteen, I had a "nervous" episode, where I was barely able to function but it went away apparently by itself after a month or two. Again it happened at age eighteen, in a novitiate that I lasted six months in and elected to go home. And in college, I had an episode in my sophomore year when I became "sick" and was unable to attend class for a week but when I came back and continued classes, I received mostly "A's." And when I started my career it was the ups and downs that a bipolar person has, but summers still seemed to remedy the dark nights of the soul. And the novitiate was God's territory. So I offered everything up. I only had one time, Christmas during the novitiate, where I exploded when I received no help in any of the dishwashing or setting of tables. Christmas morning I was so exhausted that by early evening I had to go to bed. I felt as if no one cared and I was totally abandoned. It was a case of clinical depression after a manic episode. But as often happens in a religious community, no one noticed.

After my novice year, I was sent to the seminary; immediately leaving the monastery, where I had taken my vows, for the academic world I loved so much. I had a scholarship that paid all my tuition, and the Abbot had warned me that the community needed this help, and I must keep the scholarship or I might not be able to continue. So I entered my training with trepidation; I had to keep a 3.75 average or better. I threw myself into my studies and did nothing else. Losing touch with those who lived around me, I created a shell that protected me from the outside world. No matter how dark it got, I had an aim or goal of reaching priesthood. The first semester I got a 4.0. But that just meant I had to repeat the feat the next semester so I continued to pressure myself. Until one day one of my confreres said, "You know if you die tonight the community will not put your grade point average on your grave stone." It shocked me back into reality and after that things appeared to go much better, or at least better. I felt as if I was in the "dark night of the soul," but I could survive or I would survive.

After the seminary, I was ordained. My ordination and the first years of returning to teaching went extremely well. I was able to hold my head above water as more and more positions were placed on me. As it is said in most religious communities, "If you do a job well, you will get more and then even more to do." I was chairman of the English Department, taught four classes of Freshman English, Director of Vocations, Director of Admissions, kept the full monastic schedule while having two evening study halls, and did parish work on weekends plus every other week I had daily Mass out. After five years of that, I started "to breakdown." Once again, no one noticed. I was good at hiding my ups and downs for I had years of practice. In the summer, I started to bike ride twenty or thirty miles a day. It helped until I became manic about that as well.

But as time went on I started to fall into deeper depressions and then I had these manic highs. But no one noticed because I did not. I just thought it was normal. My M.Div. degree was done in two and a half years. Eventually I totally burned out at my first monastery, and then went to a second one where I was made Director of Campus Ministry. The second monastery did everything to accommodate my illness that still had not been diagnosed. As time went on, it became more and more evident not only to the community but to myself that I needed help. I had become an associate professor of Education and was now tenured, but I kept doing more and more. It was as if I had to prove something even though the Abbot kept telling me I did not.

After sending me away for a year to England for a rest and study, that actually was a year of recuperation from burnout, I returned and fell into the exact same pattern. Finally at age sixty, the Abbot, speaking for the community, asked me to see a psychiatrist. I said yes. And the rest is part of my personal history. In fifteen minutes, the psychiatrist diagnosed me as Bipolar I with Post Traumatic Syndrome (PTS). I sat there with relief for the first time. I knew what caused me to act the way I did. It was chemical and not my fault. I openly acknowledged this illness to the community and have worked towards control ever since.

I put both of my communities through hell over the years. But I was functional, not just a little, but very functional. At times, I did do well. I was short fused. I suffered from moodiness. I was totally exhausted from insomnia. But in general, I was an active member of the community. But no one noticed, or if they did, no one confronted me on my moods and depression.

The causes of my manic depression were multiple. And it is good to look at all the various causes there are to choose from. And since depression and bipolar disorder seldom have one cause, it is first good to look at the risk factors that might have made me the way I am. There are three types of risk factors.

1. Vulnerability Factor
2. Triggers
3. Maintaining factors

Vulnerability Factor

First, there is the vulnerability factor. This does not predict when a person might become depressed or even if they ever will become depressed. But it contributes to the underlying risk that a given person will someday develop depression. My sensitivity to the world around me created a person who was a natural for depression when the world seemed against me. My anxiety about everything traumatized me. I was a prime candidate for depression.

TRIGGERS

Second, triggers help to turn this vulnerability into an actual depression. My father died when I was eight years old. When my uncle held me over my father's casket and said, "Now you are the man of the family." And I took him seriously. I asked myself how could I do that, and I became depressed at eight. Or when my mother visited my younger brother and I at the summer camp we went to, and told us that if she died during an operation later in the summer, we would be raised by Mooseheart, a charitable organization that took in orphans of their membership. And I could mention a hundred and one other triggers that sent me into clinical depression at the age of eight.

MAINTAINING FACTORS

Third, the maintaining factors that keeps a depression going when it has started. Sometimes the risk factors that started the depression stay around and mine certainly did. But depression brought a lot of additional symptoms to my doorstep. The depression became worse, but also I had manic episodes when I hit puberty. At fourteen, I would get highs and then lows that brought me to the bottom of my soul. I failed a science course in my freshman year of high school. I decided I was no good and that I would be expelled from the high school I was attending. It was so black that I even thought of killing myself for the first time. Suicide building on the depression brought me to consider death as a viable option.

Now what caused all this in a young boy who seemed normal on the outside and was having his soul eaten by something on the inside? There are at least nine categories that could account for my being prone to depression and/or bipolar disorder.

1. Genetic makeup
2. History / Experiences
3. Negative Thinking
4. Behaviors learned from childhood
5. Health
6. Non-expression of emotions within the family
7. Situations
8. Difficulties in relationships
9. Meaningless life

GENETIC MAKEUP

First, genetically I could have inherited a vulnerability to depression. My genetic makeup, my prenatal environment, and even gender may account for what took place. I had a difficult birth when forceps had to be used. My mother's family tended to be depressed; my grandmother took to her rocker at 65 and stayed there mostly until she died. My paternal side of the family drank all the time. I wonder now if it was self-medication.

HISTORY / EXPERIENCES

Second, our history causes us to be vulnerable. My first psychiatrist once told me that I had PTS (Post Traumatic Syndrome). I answered him with, "I never went to Vietnam." And then he informed me of all the traumas that had occurred in my life and how they had built up to explode to clinical depression later in my life. I could not disagree.

NEGATIVE THINKING

Third, the negative thinking that permeated my way of seeing the world. This was a mixed bag. I know I was schooled in this by my grandmother who, after my father died, came to live with us. The world was bad in her eyes. I adopted a "do not trust anyone" way of thinking that filled my brain with the fear and loneliness that she modeled. I knew I did not do what other boys did, so there was something wrong with me. I did not play baseball or football. Rather I liked some girl things; a dollhouse my father had built and given to a friend and small magical kingdoms that I built on our closed-in back porch. These attitudes made me feel guilty and created in me a "negative" view of myself that I carried to all I did.

BEHAVIORS LEARNED FROM CHILDHOOD

Fourth, behavior can be set in our minds at an early age. I always felt I was not good enough. I had to prove to the world that I was as good as everyone else. I never could. I still struggle with this even now. My mind is programmed to tell myself I am not as good as the next person. I spend a lot of my day envying other people. I am so shocked when people tell me that they wish they could be like me. Seldom do I believe them.

HEALTH

Fifth, health plays an important part in our developing lives. My physiology was basically good. But I did not eat properly at times and I had the usual illnesses of childhood. But after birth, I could not hold food down and went from 7 lbs something to just a little over 5 lbs. Everyone thought I would die. And as I grew up I was allergic to milk, chocolate, and other things, but I grew out of these allergies. Some of them have returned in my older years, but sometimes for different reasons; chocolate, not because I am allergic, but rather because of the caffeine.

NON-EXPRESSION OF EMOTIONS WITHIN THE FAMILY

Sixth, emotions were not expressed in our family. You did not touch or hug, and certainly not kiss. And boys do not cry. You held all your emotions in. "The deeper, the better" was our family motto. I was told not to cry when my father died. I became afraid of my emotions that remain right under the surface. This fear remains with me even to this day.

SITUATIONS

Seventh, situations affect our lives. Places played an important part for me, as I entered eighth grade we moved across the entire width of Chicago. I left behind everyone I knew. I had to make all new friends. It was the hardest year of my life. Sadly, I never really overcame this setback in my social life.

DIFFICULTIES IN RELATIONSHIPS

Eighth, difficulties in our relationship with others remain a factor that creates depression. I recall when my father died I was taken out of school, and when I returned no one would talk to me. When I tried to speak to someone, they would not reply. After two weeks, I told my mother and she asked the teacher about the situation. The teacher replied, "I told the boys and girls not to talk to him about his father." They hadn't talked to me because they thought the teacher had said not to talk to me at all. I always lived in fear of bullies when I was in school and for some reason I ran into them. I still remember the guy's name, Gordon, who harassed me to and from school until I changed schools in the fourth grade.

Ninth, meaning raises the point, "What is the purpose of my life?" During most of my life, this question arose and I was able to answer it. Not always well but I had an answer of some kind. Most likely that is why when I was tempted to kill myself over my lifetime; I never did because I had something to live for. It wasn't always the best answer, but I had one.

A few years ago, I went to a clinic to have a psychological evaluation determine whether or not my bipolar disorder was under control and it was. When I met with the psychiatrist, who handled my case, he said, "With all the traumas you have had I am surprised you are so normal." I guess I am just lucky or maybe my guardian angel is just a hard worker. Whatever the reason, I have survived.

Clinical depression is not something to be left unaddressed. Usually, the first episode of depression is a result of a trigger such as a stressful event, but the following episodes may occur without a stress event to trigger them. Thus, one can ask the question whether depression is a genetic predisposition that is then triggered by environmental factors. This question is rather difficult to answer since studies have been shown to support both the environmental and the biological perspectives.

Genetic research has shown that biological elements may play a strong role in depression. Individuals, who have relatives with depressive disorders, were found to be more vulnerable to depression in comparison to members of the general population. For example, there have been studies on identical twins, which share the same genetic make up and fraternal twins, who do not share the exact genetic make up. These studies show that biology is a big factor in the causes of depression. Some types of depression can be found in families in which those who get ill have a different genetic makeup in comparison to those who do not get ill. But then, it also turns out that people with this particular genetic makeup do not necessarily acquire the illness.

Thus, this is where external factors such as stress step in. In other cases, major depression may occur to those who "inherit" it, but then there are those who fall into depression without having a family history of depression.

According to Sonam Tamang, a researcher at Bryn Mawr College:

Other than such environmental or external triggers, the root cause of depression is a chemical imbalance in the brain involving the neurotransmitters dopamine, norepinephrine, and serotonin. When there are low levels of these brain chemicals, normal brain transmission of signals by the nerve cells is prevented. In the most primitive part of the brain, the brainstem, there lies a cluster of serotonin neurons. This neurotransmitter is responsible for controlling the important physiological aspects of the body. Included among these aspects are motor activity, cardiovascular activity, respiration, and control of body temperature.

This "imbalance" causes disturbances in brain circuits and is the main reason why depression can be such a debilitating disorder. Thus people remain in bed for weeks and some lose their jobs and even their families. There has been extensive research done in the past 20 years by genetic researchers in order to identify the genes that cause depression. At present, these genes have not been identified and one reason may be that several genes contribute to the problem thus confusing the conclusions. This means that each gene makes a small contribution and is therefore, hard to spot. Research continues in this field but it will probably be quite a while before any sure results will give us insight into how this part of the brain works.

Although it would be nice to say that nature creates the problem and nurture does very little to change this picture -- that would be inaccurate. Individuals who start working with a psychotherapist without taking drugs have been known to reverse the depression. This substantiates the premise that possibly depression is causing the body to respond physically rather than the imbalances causing the psychological depression. Thus the nature versus nurture thesis remains an unsolvable issue at the present time.

The statistics on depression are mind numbing. 330 million people worldwide suffer from depression of which only a few will receive proper treatment or attention, such as psychotherapy or psychiatry. Tmang puts it succinctly, "It is estimated that by the year 2020 major depression will be the world's second most debilitating disease, surpassed only by cardiovascular disease." Women with hormonal changes are more prone to depression. Menstruation, pregnancy, miscarriage and menopause may be reasons that depression is found more in women than in men. But in addition, women who frequently remain home do not have any stimulus that might break the pattern of depression and remain often unable to break the hold of this illness.

Having covered the causes of depression, a short statement on what should be done concerning treatment of this illness: As soon as possible, a person showing the symptoms of depression should seek professional help. Showing the major symptoms such as lack of motivation or enthusiasm for things previously enjoyed, should be taken as signals. Depression should be treated as a disease and not as an everyday, regular emotion. A psychiatrist is important in evaluating the patient as well as someone who will listen to the patient. Many people, including myself, see a psychiatrist for medication and a psychologist for therapy. New medication is being discovered each year and taking such medications should not be considered something to be ashamed of. Seeking help is the key to remaining alive when the depression overwhelms a person.

Most importantly when left untreated, severe depression can result in a suicide or a suicide attempt. In 2002 there were 31,655 deaths recorded in the United States. Worldwide, an estimated 900,000 suicidal deaths occur each year (World Health Organization (WHO),

2001). Although adults commit suicide, it is teenagers and adults in their early 20s who are at the highest risk for suicide. According to U.S. News and World Report, "each year, about 20 percent of adolescents contemplate suicide; by the end of high school, 1 in 10 will have attempted it, with almost 2,000 succeeding each year. About half of those who die suffer from major clinical depression."

In both depression and suicide, levels of a key neurochemical called serotonin are abnormally low. Modern antidepressants that boost serotonin levels are credited with the small but real decline in the overall suicide rates internationally.

A universal and perplexing reality is suicide's maleness. More than four times as many men as women die by suicide (although more women report making the attempt). Japan and China seem to be an exception. When men commit suicide, they often used methods that are not going to fail, such as a gun, hanging or drowning. Boys kill themselves six times more often as girls do. In 2000, the United States had 4,294 recorded suicides in the 10-to-24-year-old age group; only 632 of them were girls--this despite the fact that females are diagnosed with depression more often and make many more suicide attempts. A closer look suggests that males often experience and express their illness differently--more aggression, anger, irritability, and impulsiveness and less of the overt hopelessness, helplessness, and sadness common in suicidal females.

The information above was gathered by U.S. News and World Report and helps put into perspective the link between depression and suicide. The report further states:

These numbers reveal not only the scope of the problem but also the vast difference between the state of contemplating suicide-- also called suicidal ideation--a suicide attempt, and an actual suicide. Ideation, it seems, is part of adolescence for 1 in every 5 kids in a high school classroom. A suicide attempt, however, becomes murkier in terms of reporting: Is cutting oneself on the wrist, say, a suicide attempt

27

or a way of relieving tension? Of course, it depends on the patient. If someone is cutting herself, this self-mutilation is often serious and scarring, according to psychiatrists, but still is not attempted suicide. Researchers have found that those who cut themselves have no wish to die; no matter how difficult that may be to understand. They find that cutting relieves unbearable anxiety, somehow, or channels anger.

> What is most important, however, is the link between depression and suicide. The suicide prevention programs that are the most likely to succeed are those that focus on the identification and treatment of depression and substance abuse and that teach people how to cope with stress and manage their aggressive behaviors and feelings.

The end result of this study points out the relationship between clinical depression and suicide. Sadly, untreated depression leads often to suicide. The depressed person in the depths of his or her blackness can see no way to the top of the pit in which they have fallen. All that is seen is a life that will continue but is not worth living. Does spirituality or will spirituality help such people by giving them meaning? That is important but first we must look at the various religions and see what they teach about suicide and those who kill themselves.

Chapter Three:
Religion and Spirituality's Approach to Depression and Suicide

Most religions find it hard to incorporate the weak and vulnerable into their midst. Religion is for the strong. And even though many spiritual leaders mouth the words of their holy ones, the heart is not necessarily in their words. Many of the great religions of the world do not react well to those who are vulnerable. But spirituality is different from religion. While faith is a belief in some Higher Being, religion is an organized form of creedal statement, codification of laws, and rituals connected with worship. Theology is an attempt to put meaning into a belief system, spirituality is beyond religion and theology, closer to faith, yet not an exact fit. Spirituality has its roots in the word, *Spiritus*, and the Hebrew word, *ruah,* which is breath, the breathing in of the spirit into a person.

Therefore spirituality is a concern with matters of the spirit, but spirit is a vague word. Those who write or paint may find the origin of the concept in the time honored word, "inspiration," the time when the artist is breathed into by the Spirit, or as Christians use the term, the Holy Spirit; the ultimate Inspirer, a person of the Blessed Trinity, or in simple language, God. The spiritual, concerning the truths of humankind's nature, is often juxtaposed with the mundane. It may include faith in something beyond ourselves, as in religion, but the emphasis is on personal experience. In Christian circles, the closest idea is mysticism, that approach to God that is beyond words, but is reached by contemplation. Contemplation is a form of meditation often used by the saints. It also may be a reach for a life that is higher than one's present existence; a life that is more complex or more integrated with one's worldview, as contrasted with one that is connected to the merely sensual or earthly.

An important distinction has to be made between spirituality in religion and spirituality as opposed to religion. In recent years, spirituality within religious structure often carries connotations of the believer's faith being more personal or individual, less dogmatic, more open to new ideas and multiple influences, and more pluralistic or open than that found in established religions. It manifests in many cases the nature of a believer's personal relationship or "connection" with their God or belief system, as opposed to the general relationship with the Deity understood that should be shared by all members of that faith. It is not a communal form of belief but rather an individual interpretation or experience of that belief. The charismatic movement in many mainline Christian churches expresses this personal aspect of spirituality.

People who talk about spirituality often speak of it as outside of their particular religious belief, and that there are multiple ways to accomplish an approach to a Supreme Being. They believe that there are many "spiritual paths" and that there is no objective truth about which is the best path to follow. Some theologians refer to this as relativism, but many refer to it as "openness" to the spirit. Adherents of this latter definition of spirituality emphasize the importance of finding one's own path to God, rather than following what others say works. The way of searching for the right way to find spiritual peace is the one that seems correct to the searcher or seeker and not one laid out by an organized religion. Many followers of orthodox religions find that they are skeptical of these searches because they allow a person the freedom and possible license to form their own independent views of major concepts not in tune with the communally accepted teaching or creedal statements of their belief system.

In recent years, skepticism has grown with a distrust of spirituality as not being religion but rather an independent, but active and vital connection to a force, spirit, or sense of the deep self. The Roman Catholic Church has spoken out against what it calls "New Age Spirituality" that uses many non-Christian approaches that may lead away rather than to an orthodox Christianity. As William Irwin Thompson writes, "Religion is not identical with spirituality; rather religion is the form spirituality takes in civilization."

One way of being spiritual is achieved by structuring a life that is focused on certain objectives. Examples of this are: meditation or yogi, and Zen practices that empty one or increase one's will power. The good is to reach for wisdom, achieving a closer union to a Deity or even the universe itself, getting rid of all illusions or false ideas that the sensual world offers especially the feeling and thinking aspects of personhood. According to one expert on spirituality, "The 'Plato's cave' analogy in book VII of The Republic is one of the most well known descriptions of the spiritual development process, and thus, an excellent aid in understanding what 'spiritual development' exactly entails."

Some other experts say spirituality is something we can prepare for, but it is not something we do, but rather it is done to us. Mysticism is the best example of this. All religions have mystics or holy men and women. Mystics give us insights that religion often does not.

Another expert says, "Others say that spirituality is a two-stroke process: the "upward stroke" is inner growth, changing oneself as one changes his/her relationship with God, and the "downward stroke" is manifesting improvements in the physical reality around oneself as a result of the inward change."

One example from the Christian stance is St. Francis who grew beyond himself into a holy man of infinite stature speaking to God and carrying the wounds of Christ (stigmata). He gave up all earthy wealth after his experience of God and in his new found poverty gave complete service to the poor. His radical change could not be lived by the friars who followed him. His rule was changed even before he died but he was changed by his spirituality or contact with God. Another example is the Dali Lama who fled his country, Tibet, having achieved great holiness, arrived in India and built a city of exile for Tibetan Buddhists. His spirituality is not just Buddhist but he has reached out to all faiths. One book he has written is entitled *Buddha and Jesus*, in which he shares his spirituality that surpasses his denomination and reaches into the hearts of people of multiple ways and beliefs.

One final aspect of spirituality is not uniformity but rather diversity. All men and women are one, what we see is just the surface of a person, our hearts are one, and only through the recognition of this belief will the world around us actually change and become a new creation.

Now, we will look at religion and its attitude toward suicidal depression. Religion will be studied with the spirituality that the religion offers, but also spirituality that is independent of religion or is a composite of a person's search or seeking for meaning in his or her life.

Three major religions had their births in the Middle East:

1. Judaism
2. Christianity
3. Islam

JUDAISM

If one looks at the history of the Jewish people, suicide is a rare occurrence. Three acts in the Jewish faith were proscribed: to deny

God; to commit incestuous acts; and to kill oneself. Those who killed themselves were thus denied a proper Jewish burial. They were even not allowed the rites of grief. One was allowed to risk one's life to save another, even if it was certain to end in death. Another exception to the rules against suicide was when one killed himself/herself to avoid disgrace through captivity or torture. Examples of this are found in the Hebrew Scriptures: Samson (in the Book of Judges); Saul (in the first Book of Samuel); Abimelech (in the Book of Judges); and Ahitophael (in the Second Books of Samuel). But they are the exceptions rather than the rule. Later like every society, the Jews became more urbanized and secularized. Even in the centuries after the beginning of Christianity, depression and suicide became more commonplace. Eventually the Talmud, with an increasing number of suicides within Jewish society, had to condemn those who took their lives.

CHRISTIANITY

Christianity, being an offshoot of Judaism, had the same original characteristics. But suicide played a part even in the passion of Jesus: Judas Iscariot hanged himself after betraying Jesus. His representation in scripture was always that of a traitor to the Savior. Only in the second or third century did Gnostics change him into a hero who afforded salvation to mankind by arranging Jesus' death. But this is not in the canon of scripture and is a later adaptation of the story to glorify Judas as holding a secret message: the actual pawn of God who needed Judas to accomplish salvation.

Martyrdom was common for the early Christians. If one reads the various accounts or martyrologies of Christians such as Perpetua and Felicity, it is hard to distinguish between someone taking a person's life and one's taking one's own. Martyrs often, such at St. Genesius, jumped into the Circus Maximus and died for Christ. So martyrdom could be a form of suicide if looked at devoid of its religious overtones. Most martyrs were given the chance for freedom and they elected rather to die for Christ. It was only in the fourth century that Christian teaching came to view suicide of any type as evil, and killing oneself came to be viewed as no faith in the God who made humanity.

It was St. Augustine who eventually formulated the teaching of the Church concerning suicide. He wrote that the fifth commandment "Thou shalt not kill," applied to killing others as well as oneself. Thus a person who kills himself/herself is a murderer. And therefore the action is condemned as a grievous sin and one who kills himself goes to hell. From that time on, the Church embraced the teaching of Augustine and added on rather than subtracted from his teaching.

Many church councils, starting with Arles in 452, reinforced St. Augustine by officially stating that whoever kills himself/herself is a murderer. The Council of Braga stated that no Church rites could be dispensed to a suicide. Surprisingly there were exceptions: voluntary martyrdom, self-inflicted death through an act of asceticism (for instance, starving oneself to death for Jesus), and the suicide of a virgin or married woman to preserve her virtue. At the Council of Toledo in 1096, the Church decided to excommunicate anyone who killed himself/herself. Excommunication removes a person from receiving the sacraments, but if the person is dead it seems to be ridiculous to excommunicate the person. In 1096 at Nimes, burial was denied to anyone who killed themselves. Horrific customs developed after this such as dragging a body of a suicide through the streets and burying them at the crossroad with a stake driven through their body and a stone placed over their face. This seems to be the origin of ghost stories. It appears all this was done to a suicide so they would not return as a ghost and haunt the people left behind. This may have been a fear that others may have caused the suicide to commit the act of killing himself/herself. There seems to be an early, though not explicit, understanding that suicide might be caused by factors other than an intentional act on the part of the person committing the act, such as situational depression caused by intentional mistreatment by others.

All these customs continued throughout the Middle Ages. None of these sanctions prevented suicides from occurring. They still did, but often they were covered up. A hanged person was taken down and treated as if he died of natural causes, as impossible as that seems it was done. It did not even stop mass suicides from taking place. The Albigenses, a heretical group, committed mass suicide rather than fall into the hands of the Church. Five thousand people killed themselves in 1218. Even saints tried to kill themselves. One author claims that Joan of Arc did this while in prison, but failed. It was one of the reasons why she was burned as a witch. Whether this is true or not, many other saints were plagued with thoughts of suicide.

Thomas Aquinas was the final major theologian to speak on the subject during the Middle Ages. He based his theory on natural law. Suicide was wrong because it was an unnatural act. And since life was a gift from God, man did not have the right to take his own life, for it was not his to take. Dante backed this up by creating a fictional Inferno that conveyed something not found in Scripture, but only in Dante's head. Many Christians even today hold their visualization of hell and what it will be like, not from Scripture, but from the fictional representations found in the works of Dante.

The renaissance and reformation did change the attitude toward suicide on the upper levels of society, nobility and intellectuals, where there seems to have developed a more sympathetic view. But Martin Luther and John Calvin continued with a strong Christian condemnation of suicides. Only Robert Burton in his book, *Anatomy of Melancholy* (1621), actually asked the question whether someone who took their own life would be condemned to hell forever. He believed long before anyone else that those who suffered from depression might not be responsible for their actions.

Basically the Christian church has continued to condemn suicide, but over the years the stringent attitude against the act itself has been tempered by a softening of the official church. The old rules of burial outside the church yard have been removed by all the Christian churches except for some conservative mainline churches. Often such fundamentalist prescriptions are not the Churches, but that of individual pastors. One student told me that her Lutheran Church still does not allow someone who commits suicide to be buried in their churchyard, but that is the exception to the rule.

When I was a child, an uncle of mine committed suicide, and the Roman Catholic pastor refused to allow his casket to be brought into the church and burial was forbidden in the Catholic cemetery. This has changed since Vatican II. One Christmas, in the church I was serving in, the man who gave the church its Christmas tree, took his life. He was buried after a Mass in the Catholic Church. I think the story told of Jean-Marie Vianney, a Catholic saint and parish priest, is very apropos to this chapter. One day he was walking across a bridge and a woman was looking into the water and crying. He stopped to find out what was wrong. She told him that her husband had jumped off the bridge and died. She was afraid he was in Hell. His answer was "No, he asked forgiveness the second before he died." But for most people, forgiveness is not necessary since the person who has killed himself/herself has already gone through hell, and there is no need for further punishment.

The changes in Christianity and its attitude toward suicide can be seen in one church's attempt to understand or be understanding to those who take their life and their families. This change of attitude can be seen in *The Catechism of the Catholic Church* (1997) when it teaches that "Grave psychological disturbances, anguish, or grave fear of hardship, suffering, or torture can diminish the responsibility of the one committing suicide." This is a change of attitude from before the Second Vatican Council. Although the statement in the catechism does

36

not give permission to commit suicide, it does point out that for most people it is not a choice, but often an illness or fear that causes one to contemplate suicide and/or act upon one's intention to kill one's self. Although this is a statement of the Catholic Church, most other Christian churches would agree with this statement. The culpability of a person is diminished by his/her state of mind. Very few people clearly choose to kill themselves without serious cause. Recently a priest in a Catholic newspaper disagreed with this statement and wrote an article saying this was not true. From my own experiences, I have found it very true. People kill themselves when they are no longer able to make a rational decision. In order to commit a serious sin, one must be completely able to make a rational decision with a sound mind. As one author said, a person must turn totally away from God by knowing what they are doing and then decide to do it.

Suicide is not a rational act completely free of any confusion of mind. I believe that this statement by the Catholic Church is a tremendous step in accepting that suicide is not an absolute sentence to eternal damnation, but rather in most cases an act of desperation when a person sees no other option but death.

Even assisted suicide may be committed out of fear or the inability to conceive or live through a painful death. Can a person who is faced with a long terminal illness and often what seems like a meaningless period of waiting for death make a totally rational decision? Some cannot. Fear is a motivating factor. God alone can judge a person and their motives. A person may appear rational on a television stating why they want to die, but what appears may not be the true state of a person's mind. No one, not even the Church, can condemn a person who ends their life to either a funeral or Christian burial. God is the ultimate judge of such actions. The Catholic Church now seems to agree.

Islam

With Islam, our last Middle Eastern religion, we find that no other religion is more condemning of depression and suicide. Mohammed taught that God (Allah) has given each man his dignity. This fate is called Kismet. Because life is a gift from God; God alone can determine man's hour of death. One part of the creed of Islamic belief is that man must always subject himself to the will of God. Thus suicide is a very serious sin against God, worse than murder. There are two major obligations that fall upon man: gratitude to God for the gift of life and submission to Allah. Suicide is not allowed no matter what. When I went to Boston to write this book, I had a Muslim taxi driver who asked what I was doing there. I told him about this book and received a twenty minute homily on the reasons why it was the worse of all possible sins to kill oneself. When I replied that some people in a state of depression see no other way to go but death, he stated that depression can be controlled without medication and there is no excuse to kill oneself. The argument of Islam was deep within this man's soul, He said no true follower of Allah could nor would kill himself.

In questioning the role of suicide bombers in recent Middle East conflicts, the important point is the despair with which these individuals see their world. If they feel like they are powerless and feel that nothing will change, then suicide seems to be the answer to such hopelessness. Their death would be a valid way of correcting such evil and thus in tune with Allah's will. The action is therefore seen by them as religiously correct.

Muslim countries have a much lower rate of suicide than Christian countries. It seems to be the same as the ancient Greek philosophers who accepted suicide for honor or oppression. It seems that once Muslims immigrate to other countries, the rate of suicide rises. An example of this is the Turks in Germany where they still are below the rate of their Christian hosts, but not as low as if they had remained in

Turkey. Also, resident aliens frequently suffer higher rates of depression that lead to suicide.

Thus it appears that Middle Eastern religions have been unaccepting of suicide. Only in recent years has this attitude changed for the Jewish and Christian religions. The Islamic faith still is not sympathetic generally to those who kill themselves. Surprisingly the psychotherapist and psychiatrist have found it hard to enter into dialogue with any of these faiths. It is only in recent years that this has begun to take place, but it still has a long way to go. The key to this absence of dialogue may not be entirely religion's fault. Often the psychiatrist or psychotherapist, especially those trained in Freudian psychology, have been taught that ethically they must remain objective and that a dichotomy exists as to when and how to intervene spiritually.

As we move to Asia, we find religions that have usually been more accepting of suicide:

1. Hinduism
2. Buddhism
3. Japanese Religion (Shintoism and Buddhism)

HINDUISM

Hinduism does not have the negativity that the West has on suicide. *The Veda Books* permitted suicide on religious grounds. But the *Upanishads* strongly condemned suicide. So a conflict existed in the Hindu scriptures. And therefore Hinduism allowed *suttee* or widow burning until recently. Even though condemned in 1892, it is still said to take place today.

Suicide by starvation has been accepted by certain religious groups in Indian society. This is called *sallekhana*. It is performed as an ascetic practice. Mahatma Gandhi did a hunger strike to change the British colonial mind and it worked. Many other religions and religious groups have taken on this practice.

While in India, I observed that Hindus tend to be open to all religions. A dilemma for Catholics in India is one that seems to make Catholics exclusive but not inclusive. Christmas Midnight Mass, an important Catholic service, has to have tickets for the parishioners because otherwise the Church will be filled with Hindus and the parishioners would not be able to find a seat. Recently a fundamentalism has been growing in parts of India, a Hinduism that is unaccepting of other beliefs. But this is not the normal Indian attitude to other religions. They are often involved in dialogue because of their openness. For example, Dom Bede Griffiths who founded a Catholic Benedictine ashram, modeled his prayer times on Hindu forms of meditation. Later, he composed a Eucharistic prayer for the Church in India that includes many of the Hindu rituals, such as the use of the lotus flower and the marking the foreheads of those who attend the service.

In addition, the sacredness of all creation is important to the Hindu. One cult or sect of the Hindu religion, the Jains, does not allow any creature to be killed. The believers cover their faces with masks so that they do not even accidentally swallow a bug. This extremism is a sign of the great reverence that the Jains have of all creation. At this place of worship, the fish ponds are so filled with fish that one wonders how long it would be before the fish could not fit into the reflecting pools. When I visited a Hindu Temple , the Brahmin guide told me, "We have four thousand gods, but they are all the faces of the one God."

BUDDHISM

From the very beginning, Buddhism considered suicide to be proper under certain conditions. But a person had to exclude all human ambition before the individual could kill himself. The best sacrifice of oneself would be to free oneself from one's own existence.

This can cause some strange things to happen. As Nils Retterstol writes: "It may be better to give one's body than alms. Consequently it could be more praiseworthy to burn one's own body than to light lamps at a shrine." These statements require much thought before understanding. It incorporates the Buddhist concept of mind over matter.

Chinese Buddhism had a set of special reasons or motives for suicide. If a government official disagreed with a policy, he could kill himself to call attention to the wrongness of that policy. If a general lost a battle, he was to kill himself. In fact the emperor would send him a yellow scarf with which to hang himself. But even with these exceptions, the Buddhist view of suicide was still more negative than positive. Life was filled with suffering and pain and it was the duty of man to suffer these things. If a person took his own life, it would be difficult to be reincarnated. Confucius created a code of living and not a religion. He based his laws on the family and you did not kill yourself because your life was a gift from your parents and you would dishonor them. You could only kill yourself to show loyalty to your parents or society.

JAPANESE RELIGION (SHINTOISM AND BUDDHISM)

Japanese religion placed suicide more at the center of its national religious tradition than any of the other Asian religions. Japanese religion is a combination of two religions: Shintoism and Buddhism. Shintoism tends to be a life embracing religion. Many Japanese use their rituals as initiation ceremonies, for example, to celebrate births and weddings. Buddhism, on the other hand, has ceremonies that many Japanese use to bury the dead. Recently, many Japanese wish the externals of a Western wedding, having a traditional Japanese Shinto service afterwards.

Japan ritualized suicide. It created very complex rituals for killing oneself. The two traditional rituals that most foreigners know are *seppuku* and *hara-kiri*. The former was actually committing suicide on the battlefield rather than being captured, while the latter was suicide in private. Enough films have pictured *hara-kiri* that it has been romanticized into a form of ritual that probably it was not. Even though it was outlawed in 1868, one modern visitor to Japan says that if you visit hospitals even today you can see people who have been unsuccessful in their attempt to kill themselves. This experience of failed *hara-kiri* would certainly take the romanticism out of the act.

After World War II, the Japanese were secularized by the Americans. Recently, I asked a young Japanese student who had written a paper on Buddhism for one of his classes, "I did not know you were a practicing Buddhist." He said, "No. Japan has no religion." I further questioned the student and he answered, "When the Emperor, who was a god, led us into War and lost, we no longer believed in him. Now we have nothing." This was how one young Japanese male saw religion in his country. When the Emperor of Japan died, the St. Martin's University in Washington wanted to hold some kind of service and asked if they wished one. The Japanese students were mystified by this request. Why did we want to honor the Emperor? The service was not held.

When our Japanese students came to America to study, it was the first time they had ever been to a church service. At first the students found the liturgies alien but interesting. Some students even became religious studies minors or majors because they wish to learn more about religion. Actually in Japan it does not make any difference what your college degree is in, as long as you have one so there is freedom for what one would like to study.

Japan has become the country with the highest suicide rate, although China is running neck to neck, in the world. Sadly, young people are easily depressed by the loss of job, the failure to gain entrance to a Japanese University, or the inability to be who they are because of societal pressures. Devoid of spirituality, the Japanese have to struggle to find something that gives meaning to their lives. Other countries have exported Zen Buddhism and Zen meditation into their spiritual practices or religion to give depth or meaning to their lives. Sadly, most Japanese find these routes alien to them. The lack of meaning and absence of spirituality in Japan has proved to be a vacuum that sometimes suicide has filled.

When I was preparing this book, a Jesuit priest asked me, "Are you going to cover the religions of primitive cultures in Africa?" From what I have read, it seems as if some of these religions allowed suicide for the same reasons that Greek philosophers and other religions allowed it. But the high conversion rate in Africa to Islam and Christianity has changed this attitude. The rate in Africa appears for this reason to be low. As the countries of Africa industrialize and urbanize, the rate of suicide will probably increase.

Today, many people take part in a religion or certain rituals from a religion, and piece together spirituality for their own needs. This may differ from the religion itself or it may not. Some people may practice spiritual exercises that seem alien but are accepted such as Zen meditation or Enneagrams. This does not exclude a person from their religion but may allow the individual practices that increase their spirituality even though not officially approved by their religions. For example, Ennegrams are originally found in the Sufi sect of Islam but have been adapted by many Christian groups for retreats as a personality inventory. Meditation has always been an accepted way of searching for God that has various forms that allow members of various religions to practice and create their own spiritualities or spiritual practices.

Spirituality is a broad umbrella that includes diverse ways of searching or seeking some higher power. Within or without a religion, it can and does give meaning to life for many people. Meaning in life often deters suicide. When a person says, "My life has no meaning." The statement can mean "what purpose do I have in my life or why should I go on existing this way?" Meaning can be found in so many areas other than religion or spirituality. But as society becomes more financially well off and technologically proficient, there seems to be for some people, an emotional poverty that develops. Despair or hopelessness seems to be the fruit of depression caused by a society that does not value the spiritual. Without meaning, life is hopeless. Other things can cause thoughts of suicide: illness, poverty, and mental illness. All of these things from illness to meaninglessness can or do frequently give birth to clinical depression. Severe depression walks hand and hand with temptation to suicide.

There is no simple answer as to why a person commits suicide.

Certainly clinical depression is a major cause connected to the quality of life or despair that things will not get better. Sadly, it is hard for those around a person to know when that person considers life not worth living. Spirituality may act as a tool for a person to find a meaning in life once again.

What role spirituality or religion plays in forestalling suicide is a question that may not be answerable. A person who is successful in committing suicide often leaves nothing behind to say why he/she committed the act. Their families and friends are left in the dark, and even their therapist may not know why he/she did it. If a person is unsuccessful, he/she may still try again and succeed. There will be no answers in the next chapter; only insights and examples that may open the eyes of those left behind.

It would be nice to say that a person could be given a meaning for their life simply by introducing them to some sort of spirituality. But it is not that simple. In the next chapter, cases and examples will be given of people who killed themselves or attempted to do so. These are not definitive examples, nor is this a research project. These examples are merely examples. Examples do not make a scientific study. They are only what they are, insights into what other people have gone through and have either won or lost the battle.

Chapter Four:
Those Who Die and Those Who Live:

From the Viewpoint of A Spiritual Counselor
[Father Benedict Auer, O.S.B.]

While I was in the seminary studying for the priesthood, I became friends with a monk from another Midwestern monastery. He was a tall, nice looking young man who had served two or more years in the navy. He had come back from the navy and joined the monastery that ran the high school he had attended. We would walk every day. He lived in the room next to mine in the monastery where we were studying. We talked as we walked each evening after dinner around the campus. We talked as we struggled to do our papers. We discussed our classes, what we liked and what we didn't. We shared our fears with each other. He had a monk from his monastery studying with him at this time, but it was I with whom he shared with and not his fellow monk.

His monastery was different from mine. He had joined a daughter house of an English Abbey. Although they had roots in England, they had adapted well to America. His problems were the same as most of the visiting monks who were studying at this seminary. The schedule

45

was difficult. Morning Prayer was early in the morning, very early. He found it hard to make Morning Prayer and frequently missed it. For this he felt guilty. He found the studies difficult. He was not a scholar and papers were hard for him to write. So I read many of them and corrected them or suggested corrections for him to make. As we walked and talked, he discussed his moods. He was often up and then often down. I shared my own mood swings with him. I did not know I was bipolar or manic-depressive at the time. I would go manic while writing a paper, and then sink into the abyss of depression afterwards. I had gone to the nurse and asked for something for my nerves and he had given me valium. I suggested the same for him. I found they did not work for me because I felt drugged so I stopped taking the pills. Whether he went to get medication, I do not remember. But I know we talked about it.

He was very pious as I was at the time. Some of our courses seemed to be attacking our belief system. In our New Testament class we were told that the gospels were not literal and both of us had problems with that. Now I realize what exceptionally good classes they were. His self-esteem was low, but who was I to talk. Our friendship got stronger as the year went on. He told me at the end of the year that he was moving into the seminary hall out of the monastery the following year. I had only six months left to go so I would see him seldom during that time. When I did he seemed fine.

I finished up and went home to teach before my solemn vows and ordination. I always remembered his birthday, it was December 8, the feast of Immaculate Conception. So I addressed his card that year. I had stamped the envelope. Then I went down to the bulletin board of the monastery and looked up and read that he had killed himself at the seminary the day before. I could not believe it. I gather he hanged himself. He had everything to live for, at least I thought so. He had nothing that I could see that told me he was a potential suicide. Maybe I had not listened, so I felt guilty. Why had I not caught the fact that he might kill himself? Did I not truly listen? What happened between our year in the monastery when we shared everything and were so close? Or were we close? I no longer knew. He was not much different from me. We both had mood swings. Both of us struggled with them, yet he killed himself.

He was a fine monk. He tried to live his monastic life. He shared my spiritual values. We both had a spirituality that was true to our beliefs. He had been raised a Catholic from birth. His mother had remarried, but so had mine. We both had stepfathers, but neither of us found that a problem. He struggled but we all do. Somewhere he lost meaning in his life. Something went wrong and I never found out what it was. Our monasteries were in different congregations. I knew no monks from his monastery whom I could ask. All my questions went unanswered. I could not attend the funeral, I was too shocked. My question was, and is, why did he kill himself and I did not.

It is a question that has surfaced over and over again in my life.

When I was most depressed and I thought about killing myself, I cast the thoughts out of my mind. Why didn't he? I started having suicidal thoughts when I was fourteen years of age and these happened on and off to the present day. They have almost completely disappeared, but once in a while they surface. A few years ago, when I was getting off an antidepressant, I fell into a deep depression. The thoughts were dark and suicidal, but I struggled against the thoughts and survived. During that time, I went to our community nurse and told him I was plagued by these thoughts about killing myself. His reply was simply, "Don't do it." And I didn't. In writing this book, one of the main questions that have surfaced is why do some people kill themselves and others do not. I wish I could tell you an easy answer but I can't.

According to many doctors and heath care workers, spirituality is an integral part of one's holistic wellness. If this is true, spirituality can affect those who suffer from clinical depression or are suicidal. Due to its general nature and personalization, however, spirituality can perhaps be better understood by highlighting key concepts that arise when people are asked to describe what spirituality means to them. Research has appeared in the *Journal of Advance Nursing* entitled "The concept of spirituality in nursing theories: Differing world-views and extent of focus," by D.S. Martsolf and J.R. Mickley, professors of nursing at Kent State University. The article lists the following areas as the major concepts that concern people with regard to spirituality and illness:

* Meaning: significance of life; making sense of situations; deriving purpose.

* Values: beliefs, standards and ethics that are cherished.

* Transcendence: experience, awareness, and appreciation of a "transcendent dimension" to life beyond self.

* Connecting "increased awareness of a connection with self, others, God/Spirit/Divine, and nature.

* Becoming: an unfolding of life that demands reflection and experience; includes a sense of who one is and how one knows.

Although these concepts were originally designed for hospice care, they fit the major thesis of this chapter, namely, the influence of spirituality on depressed and suicidal persons. With these points in mind let us go back to the first example.

It would seem that the individual who killed himself had all of these things in his spirituality: meaning, values, transcendence, connecting, and becoming. He was going on for the priesthood and was to become a fully professed monk. He had a purpose and he knew it. His values were based on the ethics of the Church and he held to his standards. There may have been a glitch in his armor during the year I was away. He was living in the seminary instead of the abbey. He might have gotten involved in something that went bad: drugs, sex, or some other sinful activity, but I doubt it. And he was so upset and ashamed that he felt the only way out was killing himself. It is possible. He certainly fulfilled the other two criteria. He felt at least at one time close to God and seemed willing to learn who he was. But do any of us ever know who we are. Therefore his death is a mystery. I do not believe there was any note. I often think of him, realizing how close we were, and yet I did not know he was hurting somewhere deep inside.

In 2005, I did a wedding for one of my former students and his fiancé. Both of them I had met before the wedding a couple of times. During one of our meetings, I mentioned I was bipolar. His fiancé was very pleased I had said something because she said her brother suffered from manic-depression. And so we finished the preparations and I waited for the wedding. The wedding took place at a beautiful garden outside of Bend, Oregon. I thought I was going to stay at a hotel but then the bride's family asked if I minded staying with them. My former student said "The house is quite nice." He was a quiet young man but I never had anyone understate something as he did. The house was magnificent. The house stood on a ridge overlooking the entire valley. Long outdoor patios circled the side of the house that faced the mountains and national forests. It was a breathtaking view. I was given a room that served as the bride's mother's art studio. It was better accommodations than a five star hotel.

The family was just wonderful to me. There was the father, who after selling his computer business, had built the house and was now pursuing a photography hobby. His photos were beautiful. He had just recently returned from Nepal and there was a photo in his living room that was so beautiful that I wanted a copy of it. I did not have the courage to ask for a copy until afterward when I logged into his web site and found a collection of his photos from Nepal and asked if I could order some and he said "Just tell me what you want and I will run them off for you." I now have three of his photographs: one large and two smaller that hang in my office at the University. And everyone comments on their beauty and artistic settings. The mother was an artist and so caring it was almost embarrassing. Monks are not used to be taken care of so well. The bride and her soon to be husband stayed at the house.

Finally there was the bride's brother who had just graduated from an Ivy League college. He was bipolar. A brilliant student who had suffered from manic depression and was now hearing voices. He was heavily sedated. He had been recently institutionalized but was now out. He functioned, but very poorly. He could not keep a conversation going for very long. It had been at least his third institutionalization. Sadly, he was going deeper and deeper into depression.

If love alone could save someone from clinical depression, this family could and would have done it. They loved him unconditionally. When he acted strange from the medication they accepted it. They asked him what he wanted to do and when he said nothing, they accepted that. They never forced him to do anything, but take his medicine. They allotted his pills and waited until he took them. They saw that he ate and that he took care of himself. No matter how he acted he was accepted as part of their family. I was so impressed by this concern and love that I felt the young man would get better over time. It would be slow, but it would work.

The day of the wedding, the family asked him if he wanted to come and he did. He was to be a groomsman so he asked not to take his medicine or his family decided he shouldn't. Whatever it was, it worked. He was a young man who was unmedicated, not the one I had seen at the house, but a fun loving and sweet person. He was a brilliant kid who had three or four potential articles almost ready for publication and he had only just graduated from college. But his mind was cycling rapidly and the depression had become so deep he could not handle the pressure and broke down. But for the wedding he was so great.

The wedding went well and I rode home with the young man and his father. The young man had been drinking. I told the Dad not to give him his meds because with that much liquor in him there would be a reaction. The next day before I left I talked to Mark and told him to keep up his courage. It would be a fight but it was worth it. I rode home with the groom's brother and his girlfriend. It was an enjoyable ride and I told them how impressed I was with the family and how much love there was that I had seen. I said that I, being bipolar myself, thought that Mark would make it. I had never been that severe but it just took time.

After I arrived back at my monastery, I had him on my mind a lot. I had contacted the family once and all seemed to be better. Then some weeks later, I got a phone call from my former student's mother that the young man had killed himself. She had no details, but he was dead. I was so moved I wrote a couple of poems so they could share them with friends. Later I found he had jumped off a Portland bridge and drowned. Sadly, all the love in the world had not saved this young man's life.

He seemed to have lost all when he lost the ability to be who he knew he was. Without that ability there was no reason to go on. In addition, he saw that the quality of life he had before his clinical depression and his drugged state that he had afterwards was drastically different. He no longer felt he could become what he had envisioned for himself. His research had not led to his breakdown; rather he broke down in the midst of his research. His future looked as bleak as the present, and the present was nothing but the inability to think and respond to the normal pleasures of life. This was not a one-time thing, but rather something he felt would go on and on. I have told the story from my viewpoint. I would like to share, with the permission of his parents, a letter his father wrote. The letter to his friends and myself that states the story of this young man so well:

Hello, friends -- you have either explicitly asked to learn more about Mark's illness, or I have presumed that you wish to know... Feel free to share this, but please take care that we celebrate Mark and not dwell too much on his suffering.

As you might know, Mark struggled with bipolar disease. He had a number of manic episodes in the past six years, most requiring hospitalization when his thinking became too disordered. His medications would be changed and, after a few months of recovery, he would be back at Dartmouth continuing his studies and living among the community he absolutely loved.

This past May, after three episode-free years, for some reason Mark again began a manic phase. Martha and I met him in Washington, DC for a fun week of exploring that great city. We explored that city's great landmarks and our country's history (Mark's third or fourth time), watched the Nationals win an important baseball game; ate great food; dreamed how Mark's "brain-imaging" papers would be in the Library of Congress someday – in short, we had a great time. Afterward, he and I spent three fabulous weeks driving back to Oregon. But, despite taking his meds, being on a relaxing trip, and finally being in his other favorite place, Oregon, his mania slowly grew. New doctors were engaged, meds were changed, he was hospitalized at one point, and yet Mark could not quiet his mind. It was a heroic effort -- there wasn't anything suggested that he didn't try. At last, Mark gave up almost complete control of his life in order to try to get better ... and he wasn't getting better. His racing mind and disordered thinking were closing him off from everything that he loved. His life was getting smaller and smaller -- just the opposite of the life that he knew and that you all knew of him. Whether at a moment of clarity or pain (I suspect the former), Mark decided "enough already"; he borrowed a car, drove three hours to Portland from our home in Bend, Oregon; and leapt from a bridge toward the night-lit skyline of his beloved city....

His professor at Dartmouth College wrote a marvelous eulogy for Mark, who had been his senior honors thesis student. Dr. Peter U. Tse captures the loss of such a talented young man and the questions that he left unanswered, but also touches upon his spirituality:

I first met Mark in my course on perception in the Spring of 2002. About a year later he took my small seminar on the evolution of the human brain and mind. He became interested in understanding why the human mind can break down in ways that the minds of other animals do not seem to. Our closest relatives, the chimpanzees and bonobos do not seem to suffer from such afflictions as schizophrenia or bipolar disorder. Moreover, the expression of schizophrenia is a pretty constant one percent of the population throughout the world. This suggested to him that schizophrenia and perhaps certain other mental disorders are in evolutionary terms relatively recent phenomena that may be closely connected to the evolution of the human mind. He read a paper by a scientist named Tim Crow that suggested that schizophrenia is 'the price we pay' for having human minds. Certainly there has long been a popular suspicion that there exists a link between madness and creativity. Mark decided to plumb the depths of this connection and wrote a brilliant paper for the class on the genetic and neural basis of schizophrenia. At about this time I had a hunch that a new brain imaging technique called "diffusion tensor imaging" could be used for more than the analysis of anatomy, which was its sole purpose to date. I suspected that one could look at people's brains that differed along various mental traits, such as creativity or schizotypy, and do a cross-correlation between their scores on measures of these mental traits and the anatomical differences expressed by their brains. Since it was just a hunch, I raised the possibility with Mark one afternoon after he confided in me about his personal struggles with mental illness. I told him it would be a long hard road since we would be doing things that no one had done before and there would surely be two steps backward for every three forward. He jumped at the chance and became an integral member of my lab for the next year and half, staying on a full year after graduating even though I could only afford to pay him a small amount, and working as hard and often harder than my graduate students. He opened up to me about his own struggles with mental illness even more over this time. We became friends. His passion for the project was contagious. It was in part a desire to understand and explore his own mind and suffering that fueled his drive and passion. But more than this it was his insatiable curiosity that filled him with passion. He was trying to get at the heart of the neural basis not only of mental illness and human mental suffering, but also to the heart of what it is about our minds that makes our minds so human, and so different from those of other animals. His main focus was on the neural basis of schizotypy, psychopathy and creativity. Each of these projects has yielded fascinating results and will be published this year and next. He worked himself at times so hard that I worried that he would suffer from burnout. He always said that he could relax in a cafe in Ladakh or Kathmandu after all the work was done, and feel good about relaxing too, knowing how hard he had worked and what he had accomplished. He expected and I expected that he would return to my lab after a year or two on the road to take his work to the next level. His papers will be of enormous interest to scientists, and the techniques he worked out will continue to be used in my lab and will surely be adopted by others. I knew that his other great passion was bettering this ugly world. He was struggling with the question of how to combine his love of science with his passion for the environment and progressive political transformation of our society. I imagined that he would find a way to combine these passions and become that rare scientist who does not forget society in his drive to specialization. In Puerto Rico, where my lab went on a retreat last December, we all talked at length about how to combine science and ethics and love; how to become scientists with a heart in a system that only rewards specialization, a kind of 'rational fundamentalism,' and competition. These discussions over the many delicious pina coladas that Mark would blend up for us went deep into the night on the deck among warm sea breezes, and they were driven by Mark's need to combine all of what makes us human into a single life. We all loved Mark and his way of thinking, his passion for life, truth, justice, and beauty. Like all of you, we will mainly just miss him. I think that we should not dwell so much on how his mind unraveled after leaving us. I think the legacy of his mind and work and life should be who he was when he was at his peak, struggling with the questions of what it is that makes us human, and how a person should live a life simultaneously dedicated to the search for truth and the search for justice, love, and beauty. I do not think he found all of the answers to his hard questions. Maybe there are no final answers. But his life and intensity of searching can serve as an example to all of us to go beyond the superficiality of ordinary things, to strive to find what is good and true.

Mark did not die from suicide, he died from manic-depression, the same as if he had lymphoma or leukemia. Depression can kill and it did. Mark was a spiritual person. He was not a church goer, but spiritual as Dr. Tse described him. He was a seeker of truth. He strived "...to find what is good and true." He loved the outdoors. But in the end, when his dad asked him, "Don't you see the beauty around you?" His answer was, "That is not enough," and sadly it wasn't. Sometimes whatever you do is not enough; everything is tried and everything fails. As spiritual as one is, the disease takes over and nothing helps.

There is no cure for bipolar/manic-depressive disorder. There is maintenance but sometimes the maintenance is more than a person can handle. As you have seen, the first two of these cases are young men, mainly because if men attempt to end their lives they are usually successful.

My next example is a young woman who was one of my students some years ago. She took a course I was teaching on the spiritual quest or the search for God. She chose as her topic "Spirituality and Mental Illness." In the paper, she told her story which I will share in part with you. Lisa is very open with her story and I have permission to share this with the reader:

> The reason I chose this topic for my paper, was not only because it is obviously something of such interest to me, but because I saw some of myself in many of the people we studied. Now, I am not trying to say, I am a saint, or have any delusions of grandeur. Simply that, I have had some similar experiences, and it brought forth again questions that I have asked myself often since my diagnosis of Bipolar Affective Disorder I. How would St. Hildegard, St. Catherine or any of the many others, be treated in this day and age? How would I have been treated back then? Are there great spiritual thinkers today that are locked away in institutions or being repressed by our scientific

56

and logical society? I doubt I will ever be able to answer those questions, but they have led me to want to explore myself deeper and more completely, and look at the issue on a personal level. Am I a mystic, am I mental, am I a little of both, or does it even matter?

Lisa, after writing this, went on to chronicle her life in a confessional autobiography:

I was a quiet child. Always playing quietly, reading, coloring, or playing with toys quietly. I read by the time I was four and hated cartoons, and would only watch surgeries on TV. I was indeed an odd child. It was only as I got older, that I started watching cartoons. I often would think about the meaning of life, and wondered what my purpose is? I would just sit and think about things like that. This started at about 3 years old.

Ages six to ten is the age I was first introduced to church. My mother got clean and sober when I was five. Left her abusive husband, my legal father as I am adopted, but we have no relationship. We started going to an Episcopalian church and I was baptized by choice at the age of seven or eight on Easter. My mom and I were baptized at the same time. She later left the church because of their refusal to substitute grape juice for wine for her and the other recovering alcoholics that attended the church. This ended up being a big controversy, over which they lost my mother's favorite priest. We hopped around from church to church for a couple of years, but the experience left my mother deeply hurt and scarred, and she hasn't been back to church since.

By age of 12, I had tried to commit suicide twice, once I tried to slit my throat and once I tried to slit my wrists. I am including this for a number of reasons. First of all, I believe some of the traumas in my life triggered my mental issues at this point in my life, which at the end of my paper, I will go into more details on my theories on mental illness and my experiences. Another reason, is both times, I tried to use a very, very sharp box cutter. They were my mothers, as since she was a high school dropout, she worked hard labor jobs and there were always tools about the house. And both times, I pushed down with the very tip of the razor blade as hard as I could, it hurt, my skin turned white and was indented for awhile afterward, but no matter how hard I tried, I could not break the skin. The time I tried to slit my throat, I actually cut off my air and could not breathe, but did not break skin. These were not dull razors. I was not just pushing lightly cause I was a scared little girl.

About the age of fifteen my mother and I started to explore Native American Spirituality. She had bought me a Native American meditation tape. I put the tape on in my room one day, laid down on my bed, closed my eyes and listened very closely to the words, "Oh, Great Spirit, Earth, Sun, Sky and Sea, You are inside and all around me" over and over again being chanted in a beautiful female voice and with drums and flutes in the background. I then thought I was floating in space, I saw a Native American male and female spirits. They told me to surround myself with white light and explore the galaxy, which my spirit then soared through all the planets, except Pluto, I was scared to go that far. I believe this was my first hallucination. If not hallucination, a pretty trippy dream.

My next experience is when I was 18. I went through a time when every strange experience went away. At eighteen I was living in eastern Washington, attending a community college getting my AA degree. I was living with my mom and her third husband. I was watching TV in my room one day, when I got up, went into the living room started crying and said there is going to be great devastation, it has to do with water, we have to leave, we have to move now. I remember it like a dream, like I didn't have any control of what I was doing. Two weeks later, there was a big flood in our town. Washed away bridges and roads, Red Cross and the National Guard came in to help evacuate everyone.

I met my current husband online when I was 23. Through his faith, he brought me to Christ and Christianity. I know this will sound cheesy, but our first kiss was a very spiritual experience. It was like our souls came together, the world fell away and I was totally lost within this other person. I knew we would be together for the rest of our lives and that I had found my soul mate. We were married 6 months later, and it is the best thing I have ever done.

I was diagnosed with Bipolar I disorder around November of 2003. I was blessed that I quickly became stable on medication, and have done fairly well since then. But this then raised the question, all these experiences that shaped me so much into who I am, are they all now just fake? Am I now left with nothing but a mentally ill brain, and cannot trust myself or my experiences, for fear that they are hallucinations?

I talked to pastors, friends, family, online bipolar message boards, my spouse, co-workers, basically anyone who would listen about this. I have prayed, and searched. At this point in my life, I have come to the conclusion, that I am a combination of the two, mentally ill and spiritual. I have had experiences such as those before the age of five, before I even had heard of Jesus, yet dreamt of heaven and saw angels. Was I mentally ill as a baby and very small child? If so, how did I know all the things I knew? How was I able to dream things and they happen, or predict floods in the past. How at less than a year old was I able to have a hallucination of angels, remember it as a small child, if angels weren't really there? Who am I to question such things, isn't that an insult to God, if I believe. Or is the belief in God wrong and there is nothing out there. Or, simply, later in life I hallucinated that I remembered all these things when I was younger. I guess I will never really know until the end of my mortal existence. For now, I believe that some experiences were real, such as the angels, visiting heaven, Jesus coming to me to release me of my fear, and others were hallucinations. Such as my Native American space trip. I am now in a place were I can truly laugh at such an idea.

I have left a lot out, as if I included every little thing that influenced me, we would be here for a couple hundred pages. These are the main highlights. I still don't know what religion is right for me, I still don't know if I will always be able to tell a hallucination from the "real" thing. I do know that I have no doubts to the fact that Jesus is the Savior. There is a heaven, and angels, and I have been in their presence. I do not believe this makes me special. I have no delusions of grandeur of being some important spiritual person. I am just one soul on a journey, trying to learn as much as I can. I rest on the belief that as long as I am seeking Jesus, and seeking to understand as much as I can and as much as I am ready for I will be fine. I battle fear on a daily basis, but am very aware of its effects on myself. I believe I have had the experiences I have had, to provide me with the foundation I need so that I can go out and spread the seeds and help every soul that I can possibly help. Some say, "Oh, you're a mystic!" when I tell them of my experiences. I really don't think it matters. As long as I can help others. Labels really are meaningless. Humans cannot be labeled, as there will always be exceptions to everything. Such is one of the many consequences of free will.

The medicine has helped her deal with her manic-depression. But along with medicine she has developed a strong spiritual life. She realizes she has multiple reasons to live: a loving husband, two young boys, and a growing relationship with God. She has lived in a family with alcoholism, so she, much like myself, does not drink. The medications she is taking is very important. Also she has not self-medicated with other forms of narcotics or food, as some depressed people do. Her search for God has been constant throughout her life. She has incorporated her search for something beyond herself, and this has given her meaning. Spirituality has done this, but without proper treatment it would not have been enough.

I believe in this case spirituality has helped this woman cope with her depression. Why? I do not know. It is an aid, but not an answer. For some reason, her search has given her meaning. Why did it not happen for the first two people? I do not know. One was taking no proper treatment nor medication. He probably did not know he was so sick. The illness crept up on him and he died from his depression. The second young man was totally overpowered by his illness. His spirituality was there, but his illness was too much. He too died from his manic-depression. I can only state that I do not know why Lisa and I are alive, but somehow we were never overpowered by our depression or manic states. Spirituality helped us cope. It finally was not enough for both of us. Both of us needed psychiatric help and medication, but both of us survived.

Many famous people have suffered from depression. Abraham Lincoln is one. His depression is well known. He had a melancholic disposition. He always seemed sad. He was humorously called the "pessimist." He thought about suicide and actually planned such an act numerous times in his life. He would spend a week in bed rehabilitated by his depression. How he survived the Civil War seems to be laid at the feet of manic-depression. Although horribly depressed for weeks or months at time, this would be followed by manic episodes. Not happy and enthusiastic manic episodes, but rather long nights and hard labor as President of the United States. He was a functional depressive. And people seemed to cover for him. When he was in bed, people knew not to disturb him. Such cooperation from his staff and his overly protective wife, was most helpful for him to go on being President of the United States. After the death of his favorite son, he was inconsolable. He never really overcame his death. Lincoln naturally had to handle his illness without medicine or therapist. His friends supported him, but there was actually nothing else that was available. Lincoln was not a formally religious man. He believed in a Deity, but not in a Christian God. His God was deistic and non-personal. But his presidency and previous political life gave him meaning or purpose in his life. It may have been what allowed him to remain as President until his death. His is a success story but written with his blood and suffering. I think his spiritually was his political mission in life that eventually saved the country from division and war.

Another famous manic-depressive, or at least some people think so, was Vincent Van Gogh. He was born in the Netherlands on March 30, 1853. Van Gogh quit school when he was only 15 and headed off to England in 1869. There he began a career not as a painter but as an art dealer. Van Gogh spent seven years with the firm, but became unhappy and decided to try his hand teaching at a Catholic school for boys. In the following years, Vincent went from job to job, living in various cities in Europe. Depending on his moods, high or lows, he would hold a job for a year and then go off to another when he either raged or became so depressed he was unable to stay at his job. Finally in 1880, van Gogh decided to head to Brussels to begin studies in art. During the next ten years, Vincent van Gogh painted 872 paintings. Van Gogh only sold one painting while he was alive, which was "Red Vineyard at Arles." For most of his life he was very poor, often spending his money on art supplies instead of food. All this made him feel a total and absolute failure not only an artist but as a person.

In 1888, Vincent was severely depressed and was admitted to an asylum. He was afflicted with increasingly recurrent periods of mental health problems, spending time in a sanatorium for each occurrence. As one critic writes, "His state of mind was not helped by overwork (especially as he did much of it outside in the hot sun), bad dietary habits, and dependence on tobacco, coffee, and alcohol." This almost certainly was a case of self-medication. And though nothing has ever been ascertained it seems as if bipolar disorder fits his latter years. His moods seem to have been caused by depression and his highs seem manic. While in the asylum, Vincent painted one of his best-known paintings, Starry Night. In mid-May 1890, Vincent left the asylum and spent the last few months of his life in Auvers, France. On July 27, 1890, Vincent van Gogh shot himself in the chest with a revolver. Two days later he died with his younger brother, Theo, by his side. Sadly, this genius, as many bipolar and depressive people do, ended his life before he had reached his fame.

For the last few months of van Gogh's life, he was seeing Dr. Gachet about his mental instability. Dr. Gachet was very sympathetic to Vincent, but to no avail. An assessment of Vincent's life is difficult. He did leave us enough writings in journals to inform us of the mental pain and anguish. He did get some help from Dr. Gachet but the methods in therapy were rudimentary at best. Medication was primitive. But Vincent was deeply spiritual. He actually trained for the ministry at Amsterdam University (1877). After he failed to get a post in the Church, he went to live as an independent missionary among the Borinage miners. His example was radical, and even for the miners beyond their understanding.

He is popularly known as much for his embodiment of the myth of the tortured romantic artist as for his work, which is seen as the visual expression of his life. Another critic writes: "Three of the most widespread myths about him are that he cut off his ear (it was only the lobe), that he killed himself because no one recognized his talent (in the last six months of his life he received generous accolades which he found very disturbing), and that he painted as he did because he was mad (he painted during his lucid periods)."

There is no doubt that Vincent van Gogh was obsessive in his work. But possibly researchers overemphasize his mental illnesses. Van Gogh suffered much and his paintings are haunted by a degree of "madness." But when he painted he seemed to be lucid. Why did his spirituality not help in his final days of his life? Maybe it did. We will never know. His paintings show a man overwhelmed by the world that surrounded him. Beauty appeared to fill his soul to the extent he couldn't hold it in nor could he paint fast enough to describe what he saw. At that point, he must have been unable to cope with his rapid cycling mind. Maybe his mind ran ahead of him and he could not catch up, the ultimate solution was death.

Often it takes another artist to capture the soul of an artist. I have always thought that Don McLean has done that in his song. I think it is the best song on suicide that there is. It captures Van Gogh's life as well as his dilemma as an artist. Mc Lean writes in his lyrics for "Vincent," the actual name of the song, while many call it Starry, Starry Night, the desperation of the artist:

Starry, starry night.
Paint your palette blue and grey,
Look out on a summer's day,
With eyes that know the darkness in my soul.
Shadows on the hills,
Sketch the trees and the daffodils,

Catch the breeze and the winter chills,
In colors on the snowy linen land.

I believe that, although this song is romantic and possibly inaccurate in a lot of its details, it does capture the sadness of depression. Every time I use this song on a retreat, I know that most young people will come up to me and say, "I have felt that way," or "When I feel depressed that is how I feel." Sadly the artist killed himself, but if only he had had the psychological help and medicine of today, he might not have had to die. On the other hand if he did have today's medication, he might not have produced what he did. The artist creates not just when he or she is in a good mood. In depression, often the art becomes truer and clearer, through the anguish and pain.

Many other artists have suffered as Vincent van Gogh did. Sylvia Path and Anne Sexton, both poets, and Virginia Woolf, a novelist, suffered from depression or manic-depression, and all killed themselves. Ann Sexton was a true seeker. She did not want to join an organized religion. Although born a Protestant, she remained in contact with a Catholic priest who was her friend, and an Episcopal priest, who gave her instructions in the Episcopal Church. She was very spiritual. One of her poems I believe says it all. The title of the poem is "Rowing," and certainly captures the idea of searching or seeking as these lines demonstrate:

I am rowing, I am rowing
though the oarlocks stick and are rusty
and the sea blinks and rolls
like a worried eyeball,
but I am rowing, I am rowing,
though the wind pushes me back
and I know that that island will not be perfect,
it will have the flaws of life,

Anne Sexton had all the support. She seemed to need a psychiatrist, medicine (primitive in the 1950's but something), and finally a spirituality as found in the above poem. But life overpowered her, she lost her way and then she took her life. "All poets are mad," asserted Robert Burton in his 1621 book. Burton may have exaggerated a little, but not that much. Others who have suffered from depression, but survived, include Frida Kahlo and Georgia O'Keefe, both painters, and Cole Porter, the song writer. We could go on and on, but Kay Redfield Jamison has done a study of 47 painters, sculptors, playwrights, and poets. She found that 38% of all artists report some form of major depression at one time or another, while only 1% of the major population report manic-depression, and probably 5% of general population reports clinical depression. Being an artist is a risky business. Or maybe depressed people become artists because of their depression.

Recently I read an biographical statement by the Korean singer and actor, Bi [Rain], a young man who, on the surface seems as successful as you can be, yet he wrote:

> I fell into a depression and there were times when I even felt the urge to kill myself. So I worried myself sick over it and decided that I need to go better in studies than this, so I committed myself to reading and could recover my scores [in school] to a degree.

Suicide thoughts did not end at this time, but continued when he suffered bouts of depression. He writes later, "I had to fight against loneliness. I stayed at the studio until late after everybody's gone home to compose dances and practice and at times, I was really lonely and depressed. So, the method I came up with was to practice singing and dancing in the subway and buses." Although Bi Rain is now a highly successful actor and an accomplished singer, when recently interviewed on a television talk show, I heard him say that his biggest problem is that in spite of his fame and acceptance by people. "I am still lonely." The existential angst that many modern people have. We walk lonely in a crowd. Bi Rain has his work that gives him meaning, not everyone does. He has a smile that would melt anyone's heart, but who would think that he is actually lonely. But this is the great emptiness that many people feel, as one person recently put it, "There is a hole in my soul." Or possibly it is the "dark night of the soul."

Saints also suffer from depression, although we often feel as if contemplatives, or those who give their entire lives to God, should not. They do. Both St. Teresa of Avila and St. John of the Cross suffered much anguish in their lives. Teresa has been diagnosed by recent biographers through her letters, journals and books, as having suffered from clinical depression. None of this can be proven, it is only speculation. Although she did not have a psychiatrist, she did have a confessor and spiritual director. She also had friends who helped her in her downs and when she was sick. In her writings, she surmounted her daily life with deep contemplation, or intense prayer. Without medication, she was able, by sheer strength, to live a life that was not ended by her hand, but rather continued to the painful, yet joyous end of her life.

John of the Cross was a Spanish mystic who was contemporary with Teresa. John wrote poetry that remains classic contemplative poetry to this day. It was he who coined the phrase "The dark night of the soul." Now, St. John did not mean "depression" or manic depression, but something much deeper. The complete emptying of the soul to make room for God. But the terminology stuck, and many refer to their depression as the "dark night of the soul." And it truly feels like it. I can speak from my own experience how black and dark it seems, a sky without any stars. Saints are not free from the temptation to suicide and although they do not commit it, they are subject to the same onslaught as others.

The next example I wish to use is of a monk of St. Meinrad Archabbey where I studied for the priesthood (Father Nathaniel had been ordained while I was a seminarian in 1978). Archabbot Justin was gracious enough to allow me to use the obituary because as he said " Since the obituary was a public document, I have no objection to your using it as an example." Father was a very reserved yet wonderful man. He was Academic Dean of the Seminary at the time of his death. What was so wonderful and unbelievably Christian was the obituary that they sent out. Most monasteries like families keep secret so many things. You often talk around them but not about them. The obituary read in part:

On Monday, December 31, 2001, Father Nathaniel Reeves, O.S.B., monk and priest of Saint Meinrad Archabbey, died as a result of drowning, having taken his own life. In a note left for his confreres, family, co-workers and colleagues, Father Nathaniel expressed deep sorrow, and begged forgiveness for his untimely death.

Following his ordination, Father Nathaniel pursued studies in Canon Law at the Pontifical Gregorian University in Rome, receiving the licentiate. Upon his return to Saint Meinrad, he undertook a series of monastic assignments, many of which called upon his canonical expertise. As a teacher of Canon Law in our School of Theology, he was always regarded as thorough, methodical and clear. At the request of the Archbishop of Indianapolis, he served for many years as Defender of the Bond for the Marriage Tribunal. His skills were likewise at the service of the Abbot President and the entire Swiss-American Congregation in his role as a member of the Legal Committee. In recent years, he was regularly referred to at Saint Meinrad as the canonical advisor to the Archabbot.

Father Nathaniel also fulfilled a number of administrative assignments. He served for a time as associate director of spiritual formation in the School of Theology. He then undertook the formation of the young monks, holding the position of Novice/Junior Master for a number of years.   From 1996 until his death, Father Nathaniel served as academic dean of the School of Theology.

Father Nathaniel was a dutiful, organized and dedicated monk. He was polite and gentle. At the same time, he was known for his directness and objectivity when speaking his opinions. His confreres recognized this gift in him, and affirmed it repeatedly by electing him regularly as a member of the Archabbot's Council and as our delegate to the General Chapter of the Swiss-American Congregation.

Although somewhat reserved by nature, Father Nathaniel had a group of friends—especially among the alumni—to whom he remained steadfastly loyal. This same loyalty showed itself in his relationship with his family, especially in his attentive concern for his aging father. Father Nathaniel also maintained relationships with numerous spiritual directees, not only among the students, but also among our co-workers and those coming regularly from off campus for his kind and gentle guidance.

We will never understand fully the pain and suffering that led Father Nathaniel to take the action he did. Because he was not one to burden others with his problems, Father Nathaniel carried his sufferings quietly, keeping them to himself. Even in what must have been an extraordinarily difficult time for him, he was thinking of others first. The carefully prepared instructions found after his death will help those who succeed him to carry on his work with the minimum of disruption.

Although our community is grieving deeply at the unexpected passing of one so dear to us, we find strength in the promise of God's mercy, and in the outpouring of support we have received.

Archabbot Justin, when I requested the use of this, wrote an additional note:

The decision to be straightforward about Father Nathaniel's suicide proved very good for us in one sense.

It was particularly helpful for the students in the School of Theology. I was serving as Vice Rector at the time, and was personally involved in the tragic events of the day's discovery, and in the trying days and weeks that followed.

But our students, even years later, expressed appreciation on how we handled it in the seminary. For those of us who were on the staff at the time, it helped us deal with the reality of it as well, and to admit that we were as much at a loss as to how to understand it as were any of the students.

That is exactly what St. Benedict meant when he expressed his wish that a monastery should be a family. We can all learn from this obituary that sharing one's sorrow or lack of understanding of a suicide helps a community or family to heal. Just as Mark's father shared with his family and friends his son's suicide so St. Meinrad's Archabbey did the same. Many people found this obituary as moving as I did. If I had done the same thing as Father Nathaniel did, I would want my community to share it with the world. I have never hidden my manic-depression. I have always shared it with all those around me, not as a boast but an encouragement to those who struggle as I do. It is not a secret unless you make it one, and then it is something whispered behind your back.

By being open, it provides me with a check – I cannot revert back or stop taking my medication or seeing my doctors.

The last example is one of our former Japanese students who was raised with absolutely no spirituality in secular Japan. He was diagnosed with depression, probably bipolar disorder. While he was at St. Martin's University, he suffered his first breakdown and was sent home in disgrace. He never completed his degree. He then converted to the Catholic Church. He became a Catholic and then had a breakdown once again. He has been institutionalized four times in two years. He is now trying to complete his degree in philosophy at a Catholic University in Japan. Recently he wrote he was institutionalized yet again. He has been told at one time that if he takes his medicine he can study for the priesthood. I doubt that offer still exists. But his faith is strong. He has resigned himself to whatever will happen. And he is not suicidal. He visited our university when he was well and he and I talked about the necessity of taking his medication. He realizes it but he still gets confused. He banishes all thoughts of suicide and he holds a deep spiritual faith that is rooted in meditation, the Eucharist and his Japanese culture, especially art and music. Sadly mental pain often goes beyond one's spirituality. It seems as if he is going to be okay. He may not be able to complete his degree but he seems to realize this is a possibility. His spirituality seems to be holding him together. In the Japanese culture where suicide is so prevalent, he is doing very well.

There are times where nothing will help. It seems as if the willingness to accept one's mental illness is the key to possibly winning against suicide. In contrast to the above individual, another example happened last year. A young man had given up hope in God. He held God responsible for his illness. His grandparents and family tried to help, but he just sunk deeper and deeper into depression. He came to visit the monastery as a possible vocation prospect, but he was coming only because his grandparents wanted him to come.

This young man had been raised a Catholic, but he fell away from the Church. Religion was a burden, spirituality had supposedly failed him. In the end, he refused his medication and sunk into a depression so deep that he could not go on living.

I look at all these people I have known, and I honestly cannot tell you why I am still here and they are not. I should have been dead a long time ago. Was it because I was raised a Catholic and told that committing suicide was a deadly sin? I would be risking the flames of hell. I doubt it. Was I just stronger than others? No, that is not it. Is my spirituality greater than others? No. It is the same and maybe a little less. I have learned over the years to modify my enthusiasm even in my religious life. As St. Benedict wrote, "Everything in moderation." I know multiple other people of various faiths and spiritualities who have either succeeded or failed in taking their lives, or have not tried at all, and all these people suffer from depression. Spirituality seems to help but only when it is coupled with professional help and a person willing to cooperate. Sometimes even all of that is not enough. The burden is too much. How many times in my teens and early twenties did I want to throw in the towel and say I had had enough? I cannot count the times. But I did not.

But maybe some characteristics of how spirituality can work will help in the last chapter. I would love to say that if a person goes to Mass each day or chapel each week this will mean the person will not commit suicide but it does not. I know people who have done both and still committed suicide. Telling a person that everything is okay and God is taking care of you does not work.

When I would say how depressed I was, my mother would say, "Just think happy thoughts." Or other times, she would say, "Offer it up." True, but that isn't what I needed to hear nor did it help. A true spirituality is one that deeply affects a person's perspective on life. Meditation is a key to center on the Truth or God or whatever. Centering prayer as a form of meditation works and can help one focus.

But it is not a miracle, rather it is an attempt to get control of one's life. Then the question comes up, how much control can one have in one's life? Letting go is probably better than a rigid control. One way it is stated is "Letting go, letting God." Trite? Probably, but better than holding on so hard you break.

The mind is so mysterious that one cannot guess what another person is thinking. So I have given examples of various people and how spirituality did or did not affect their suicidal depression. In the end, we have to see what we can learn from these examples and what we see as a result of our own experiences.

CHAPTER FIVE: THOSE WHO DIE AND THOSE WHO LIVE:

FROM THE VIEWPOINT OF A PSYCHIATRIST [JESSY ANG M.D.]

I have always been intrigued about the question of whether spirituality can help someone cope with depression. Though I have a belief there is a God and an afterlife, I am still not clear whether spirituality can provide immunity to a person suffering depression from committing suicide. Before I expand on this issue, let me share with you my perspective on psychiatry then and what it is now.

My psychiatric training in the '70s was neo-Freudian in nature but there was an increasing trend toward biological treatment of mental illness. At that time, schizophrenia and manic depressive illnesses were seen to be the product of an overprotective insecure mother. Most emotional disorders were viewed as being related to dysfunctional psychological development. The core dynamics were mainly the result of the never-ending conflict between the pleasure seeking instinctual drives known as the "id" and the prohibitive guilt evoking conscience known as the "superego". Psychiatric drugs were mainly confined to tricyclic compounds for depression and phenothiazine for psychotic disorders. However, these medications gave intolerable adverse side effects such as sedation and weight gain that a significant number of patients stopped treatment, resulting in worsening their depression. Some medications became lethal when taken as an overdose due to cardiac toxicity.

In 1988, a new antidepressant became available. It was the first selective serotonin reuptake inhibitor ever introduced to the United States. It was commercially known as Prozac. The drug became phenomenal in its success. I remembered a patient that had been in psychotherapy for more than 10 years referred to me for antidepressant treatment. Despite having great insight, she was still paralyzed by her depression. After taking Prozac for 2 weeks, the patient came to me and exclaimed, "It has been a long time since I had joy." People whose lives were in a black hole had been given a second life after taking this drug, this time a bright and hopeful one.

During this time, Freudian theories on the origins of schizophrenia and bipolar disorders were discarded. They are now considered genetically driven biological disorders. Psychoanalytic oriented therapy became less utilized due to its high economic costs. This was replaced by time limited psychotherapy dealing with the here and now mainly using cognitive therapy. In this type of treatment, there was a major emphasis in changing unhealthy emotions by altering irrational thought patterns. In the 80's, the biological theory of depression was still in its birth stage. At that time, the explanation for the biological theory of depression was the result of monoamine depletion of certain neurotransmitters such as serotonin, norepinephrine, and dopamine. Such depletion caused impaired neurotransmission in the nerve endings involving the limbic system. This disturbance caused the core depressive symptoms such as lack of energy, sleep disturbances, anxiety, concentration difficulties, loss of pleasure, and suicidal thoughts. It was then postulated that Prozac and the other antidepressants worked by increasing the level of these neurotransmitters as a result of blocking its reuptake to presynaptic neurons; thereby, enhancing its availability to promote neurotransmission. In the late '80s, however, a drug known as tianeptine was found out to be effective in treating both anxiety and depression. This drug disputed the neurotransmitter doctrine, as tianeptine was a serotenergic reuptake enhancer, not like most antidepressants which were serotonergic reuptake inhibitors.

New studies then came along which indicated that depression if left untreated over time, causes anatomical and functional changes in the brain. Dr. Peter Kramer in his book, entitled "Against Depression", published in 2005, highlighted certain studies that bring a new understanding of biological depression. In May 1999, a study was published at Biological Psychiatry by Dr. Grazyna Rajkowska, associate professor of Psychiatry and Human Behavior from University of Mississippi Medical Center. She reported cellular changes in neurons and glia cells in the prefrontal cortex. The prefrontal cortex is considered the gray matter behind the forehead which is responsible for higher intellectual functions and regulation of emotions, motivation, and behavior. The neurons transmit and receive signals as well as process information. The glia cells form the support system for the neurons controlling the nutrients that the neurons receive from the blood and generally facilitate the work of the neurons. Her findings indicated fewer glia cells and smaller neurons with lower density.

In June of 1999, Dr. Yvete Sheline, associate professor of Psychiatry, Neurology, and Radiology at Washington University in St. Louis, Missouri published a study in the Journal of Neuroscience which indicated hippocampal volume loss in depressed women patients. This study also inferred that the degree of hippocampal loss was related to the duration of the depression. She also published an earlier study that depressed patients have fewer serotonergic receptors in hippocampus using PET Scan studies. The hippocampus plays an integral part of the limbic system that regulates emotion as well as the storage center for verbal memory. This may possibly explain the short term memory loss associated with chronic depression.

It is believed that the hippocampus, amygdala, the prefrontal cortex, and other parts of the limbic system form a circuit that highlights the primary symptoms of depression such as sadness, concentration difficulties, lack of drive, and feelings of hopelessness. It is believed that antidepressants work by promoting new cell growth in the hippocampus by turning on genes that releases a chemical known as brain derived neurotropic factor (BDNF). This is in sharp contrast to the effect of stress hormones on the human brain. This particular stress hormone responds as a fight or flight phenomenon usually induced by perceived threat or dread. When stress becomes protracted and profound, the stress hormones are released on a continuing basis that eventually they damage both the hippocampus and amygdala. This may be influenced by genetics, early childhood trauma, and continued exposure to stressful events or crisis. The BDNF tends to repair such damage by generating neural growth in the limbic system. By giving antidepressants, it stimulates BDNF production and thereby, promotes the repair of those brain areas regulating emotion and cognition. Yet despite this advanced understanding of depression and its treatment, a great number of my patients still remain depressed. They are still considering suicide as a way of ending their ongoing misery.

I have lost patients to suicide and have wondered whether faith or spirituality could have helped stop their tragic demise. I had my own self doubts whether it makes sense to bring God to someone who is desperate and suicidal. Would it be rational to bring God to someone who does not believe in His existence? Or even if he does, if he has not developed a relationship with this higher power, would that be enough to hold on?

I recalled treating a patient in the hospital who had lost all he had and felt no reason to go on. How could I bring spirituality to someone who lost his job, his marriage, his home, and his health?

Instead, I offered an antidepressant hoping it would relieve some of his distressing symptoms which included insomnia and anxiety. Since he was suffering from chronic depression, I thought an antidepressant could restore the chemical balance involving the limbic system. This would hopefully lead to clarity of mind and a positive outcome.

This outlook was the product of encountering many patients who have been in counseling for a long period of time who remain depressed despite achieving insight and a need to change. It was only when antidepressants were given that the transformation took place. They felt better, slept well, and restored their energy and enthusiasm which they had not experienced for a long time. This then will set into motion a desire to reach out to people who had been estranged and hurt by their miserable detachment and depression. Perhaps I also gave the medication as an expedient response to a patient's sense of futility, responding to the intrinsic pressure from my own sense of helplessness to alleviate his despair. Eventually, the man left the hospital feeling better either due to the psychiatric supportive staff and medication or the fact we gave him assistance for emergency housing and after-care.

I never brought the issue of spirituality in my therapy session by my own initiative. Perhaps, it had been deterred unconsciously by years of psychiatric training that bringing religion as being part of therapy was considered a violation of psychiatric integrity and an imposition if not counter-therapeutic. The only time I would bring faith is when medication and secular psychotherapy had failed to someone who had spirituality, no matter how frail it was.

There were many occasions, I brought such spirituality to patients. By spirituality, I meant someone who has a belief in God or a higher invisible power that governs all things. With almost all my patients being Christian, I had no difficulty engaging with them in applying Christ's life and His teachings to their therapy. I would relate anecdotes from the Old and New Testament that would provide hope to help them overcome life's disappointments.

Knowing there is redemption in suffering and embracing it with love and acceptance was a worthwhile option that I imparted. Sadly, I have lost three patients despite bringing spirituality into our therapy. I had a female social worker who was very caring toward her clients, and was greatly loved because of her compassion. She had been admitted to the hospital several times due to depression and suicidal ideation. She continued to have low self esteem despite intensive outpatient counseling and several antidepressant trials. She had a great faith in humanity and had a positive concept toward God. However, this did not stop her from completing her suicide. Her loss continues to bother me even up to this day, forcing me to ask why and what if.

I had another patient who had been depressed for many years due to severe pain involving her lower back and restricted lifestyle. She believed for a long period of time that suicide was not an option. She did not want to go to hell and believed her life was a gift from God. Her faith gradually faded as her back pain continued to worsen. She eventually committed suicide.

Finally, I had a male patient who was referred to me after a failed suicide attempt by carbon monoxide poisoning. He was depressed due to a failed marriage and being unemployed. He also suffered from chronic back pain. He stated he had no reason to live and that he had done all the things he needed to do in this world and felt there was no point going on. If there was a God, He would understand. He indicated that if ever he became homeless, he would end his life. When the Social Security Office denied him disability benefits, he killed himself. Suicide became his relief to all his disappointments, bitterness, and fears.

It was at this juncture, that I met Fr. Benedict. I first met Fr. Benedict during a mass at St. Martin's Abbey in Olympia, Washington, where the Benedictine community would celebrate mass together. During that service, he gave a sermon that particularly touched me. He mentioned he had bipolar disorder and he urged the congregation to be compassionate to those inflicted with mental illness. We spoke after the service was over.

A few months later, he went to see me for treatment. It was in one of our sessions, that I asked him, "How does spirituality affect someone afflicted by depression?" I asked this question intrigued by the fact that this patient who had chosen a vocation to be closer to God is still struggling with an illness not of his choosing that brings pain, frustration, misunderstanding, and self-doubt. He responded that spirituality does help but depending on the depth of the person's spirituality prior to his struggle with depression. I then asked, "Would spirituality be enough for someone to be able to cope with the despair though his depression was biologically driven?" I probably asked the question because I was having doubts whether spirituality could help someone's resiliency against despair. This may be due to several losses that have emotionally scarred me to some degree which I have indicated earlier, as well as some personal losses that I am still having difficulty comprehending their demise.

The question was not raised again until Fr. Benedict officiated at a wedding of his former student in Bend, Oregon. He met the bride's brother who suffered from bipolar disorder. A few weeks later, the young man ended his life. This young man had a very accepting family, a great love for humanity, and a continuing search for a deep spirituality. Why then did he commit suicide? Perplexed and saddened by his death, Fr. Benedict decided to write a book pursuing the question I earlier asked. Does spirituality prevent someone from committing suicide? What degree of spirituality must a person possess to cope with depression so it does not end in despair and suicide? Fr. Benedict then asked me to research the biological aspects of suicide and what certain traits or markers would indicate whether one becomes a high risk to be self-destructive.

In most of my readings about suicide risk and depression, the following observations are generally accepted.

#1 PRESENCE OF PSYCHIATRIC DISORDER

It is known that 90% of suicide victims are due to psychiatric disorders and more than 50 % of them are due to a diagnosis of depression. Other disorders include schizophrenia, bipolar disorder, and substance abuse. But all of these are closely associated with depression. Schizophrenics become eventually depressed due to their sense of isolation, loneliness, and being constantly haunted by their delusions and hallucinations. People with bipolar disorder have a higher risk of suicide when they become depressed because of difficulty descending from euphoria to despair, as well as their depression being quite profound and disabling.

#2 GENDER DIFFERENCES

Men are more likely to complete suicide due to a higher tendency to express aggression and impulsivity, and because they have access to lethal means such as guns. Women have a higher incidence of depression and suicide attempts. However, they have a lower rate of suicide completion because they use less lethal means such as drug overdose. Also, drug overdose takes some time to bring its effect of altered consciousness, so a good majority of them is still able to change their minds and seek help. Also, women are willing to reach out and seek professional help. If not, they ask support from their friends and family.

#3 PRESENCE OF SUBSTANCE ABUSE

It has been observed that one in five suicide victims were intoxicated at the time of their death. Alcohol appears to lower behavioral inhibitions, serving as a precipitant to the suicidal behavior. It has been postulated that alcohol can induce biochemical changes similar to changes in a subgroup of depressive disorders. Cocaine and amphetamine abuse can lead to severe depletion of dopamine from the brain resulting in acute profound depression. There have been many cases of heroin and methamphetamine abusers that after injecting themselves with a heavy bolus of these drugs, they become suicidal and end their lives in a violent way.

#4 HISTORY OF AGGRESSION AND IMPULSIVITY

Dr. John Mann in a paper entitled, " The Neurobiological Aspects of Suicide" stated that aside from hopelessness and suicidal intent, impulsivity and aggression seems to be a primary characteristic leading to suicidal behavior. He also stated that people who attempt to commit suicide have been found to have lower serotonin function and those who completed suicide have the lowest serotonin levels. Postmortem findings of suicide victims from depression indicated low levels of serotonin in the human brain particularly in the limbic system and brain stem, and increased density of serotonin receptors in the neocortex. Whether these low levels of serotonin became the biological impetus for suicidal behavior or was it already present for a considerable period of time as part of chronic depressive state is debatable and subject for further research. The answer to this question will have significant ramifications for the treatment of depression. If suicide is caused by incremental neurochemical dysfunction, would all patients experiencing early stages of depression benefit by being given antidepressants to prevent the progression of depression to suicide?

#5 SENSE OF HOPELESSNESS

This is the universal feature of patients who have attempted suicide. Most research studies, including Aaron Beck, John Fawcett, and John Mann, point to hopelessness as a common denominator for suicide attempt or completed suicide. All the patients I have treated after a suicide attempt expressed this perception. This may be seen in patients who see no solution to their crisis they are experiencing such as poverty, chronic physical illness, disability, chronic pain, and loss or separation from a loved one. It is in this regard that the attribute of resiliency becomes a significant factor for hopelessness not to set in.

Resiliency is the ability to withstand adversities and life's trials, and still be able to maintain a positive outlook on life. Some people are more resilient than others. When these people face life's adversities, they have less tendency to become depressed and feel hopeless. They seem to have the strength to handle disappointments. They grieve and then move on. It is unclear why some people are more resilient than others. Some researchers indicate that resiliency is genetically predisposed just like temperament. Others believe it is nurture along with nature that plays a significant role in developing resiliency. A recent study shows that a genius does not become one just because he has extraordinary genes. It must be complemented by sustained hard work to excel and achieve one's greatest creativity. Resiliency only becomes a great shield against despair if one has been exposed to prior trials and disappointments.

Rather than placing my destiny on genetics and becoming fatalistic, I strongly believe that personal conviction, especially spirituality, can help someone deal with life's struggles before it ends into profound depression. I have encountered several personal losses and great trials in my life. And even though at times, I was greatly saddened, I did not become quite depressed to end up in profound despair. It was my faith that made me overcome these trials. I accepted as part of my creed that suffering is part of living, and that I have a God who is loving, who made me feel I was not alone through those difficult times. I have a belief that life is a transition and there is another life where I will again connect to the people I have lost. This has helped me overcome my grief. Perhaps, this has helped many holy men and women who have battled depression with a sustaining belief that God is with them, making them feel not alone and providing sustenance in their hours of darkness.

Another possible source of coping is a sense of purpose or the need to go on living. There have been many occasions when my patients have told me they were tempted to commit suicide but did not pursue it because they had a sense of obligation to live for someone or something. This may refer to their spouse, their children, their community, their faith, or a sense of duty. I had a patient who was physically and emotionally abused as a child by her parents. She never liked herself. She had to work two jobs to support her family. She spoke constantly the need to end her life to end her pain. When I asked her how God could accept her suicide, she said God would understand because God is merciful. The only reason she is still alive is because she had to care for her grandchildren, whom she could not abandon. Perhaps, this may explain how Lincoln survived his depression. He had a cause to survive his bouts of despair, which was to preserve a nation and to lead the people in a time of great crisis. This helped him cope with the loss of his two sons, the mental instability of his wife and the agony of his depression. It is also because of his abiding faith in God that he survived his depression. Jon Mecheam, author of the " American Gospel", in a TV interview in "Meet the Press", stated that Lincoln may have been the most religious president the United States ever had because his second inaugural address was like a religious sermon. This spiritual connection may not be enough for some to overcome their despair. Fr. Benedict indicated some cases where people with deep religiosity and sense of purpose ended their lives tragically. It is possible in this regard that they could have benefited from pharmacological treatments. We now have effective antidepressants, mood stabilizers, and even atypical antipsychotic medications that can relieve profound depression. Electroconvulsive treatment (ECT) is still effective for melancholic patients, particularly elderly patients who became profoundly depressed despite having a supportive environment and great spiritual connection. Vagal nerve stimulation and transcranial magnetic stimulation are new technological modalities that are now available to treat medication resistant depression without causing significant memory loss that electroconvulsive treatment usually induced.

Where does spirituality play a role in depression and despair? To answer this question, let us start by understanding placebo therapy. A placebo therapy is defined as a positive response to a drug that has no pharmacological value or as the layman calls it a "sugar coated" pill. A significant placebo response has been found in antidepressant trials. Most clinical trials involving antidepressants have a 25% to 35% placebo response rate. Some researchers have explained that such phenomenon is due to either a desperate belief in the medication to provide relief or the interaction with the research staff. This interaction can give them a feeling of not being alone and being cared for to some degree.

Is spirituality some form of placebo therapy? I believe it is much more. If spirituality is deep and tested, it will help patients become resilient; so that when a disappointment or crisis strikes, the patients will be able to accept such crisis without dread and resentment. The patient sees the crisis as a challenge that can be solved, rather than a scourge that brings fear and hopelessness. However, if a patient has depression with a strong biological basis such as recurrent depression along with a family history of depression, pharmacological treatment is strongly warranted. If not, even with deep spirituality, a person's depression will eventually reach the black hole of despair where he finds relief when life is ended through suicide.

One important aspect of surviving depression is the feeling of not being alone in struggling with the condition. This may explain the fact why people get better after a short stay in the hospital. The presence of other patients who validate and empathize with their emotional pain along with the nurturing environment of a psychiatric ward can alleviate one's emotional confusion and distress. This engagement can bring a sense of direction leading to hope and perseverance. Spirituality also provides such an avenue. I recalled a young man who told me that he was thinking of committing suicide after his father berated him as a failure because he was receiving poor grades in his classes. After having a dream, where an angel told him not to commit suicide, he woke up with a great fervor to continue on living. God cared for him.

Perhaps a deeply connected spirituality, with a feeling of being loved by others, can help overcome despair. Making use of the medications can also prevent someone from ending one's life. Despite these interventions, there is no guarantee that suicide will not occur. People end their lives because they cannot go on living because the pain, physical or/and emotional, is too much for them to bear and they see no solutions to their sorrows or fears.

If suicide then takes the better part of someone we loved, we only can console ourselves that the pain has finally ended and their death has brought peace to their chaotic mind. Perhaps, serenity can also come to us if rather asking why and what if of the unexpected death, that we make a heroic effort to remember, share, and visualize the person whom we have lost before the nightmare of depression came. By doing so, we will appreciate life again bearing no shame, sorrow or guilt.

Conclusion: No Answers, Only Questions

(Conclusion by Father Benedict Auer)

At the end of this book, I would have liked to have given the reader a package all wrapped in gift paper and tied neatly with a ribbon. But I must say I am sorry that I cannot do that. Spirituality can help some people not commit suicide even when they are clinically depressed. But these same individuals must take their medicine and see a therapist and hopefully a psychiatrist who can prescribe the proper antidepressants and/or mood stabilizers, especially if they are bipolar or manic-depressive. It is not one or the other but a combination of all three therapies: spirituality, psychological counseling, and medication that seems to work the best. The sad thing is that there is no foolproof method. As you have read, even if a person has done all three approaches, it can fail. As in our second example, Mark used therapy, he took his medication, and he was a spiritual person. In addition, he was surrounded by his loving family who supported and loved him unconditionally. If anyone should have been able to overcome the illness of depression, he should have if the formula worked. But no one can change one's genes or predisposition. No one can blame themselves for any of this. This book is absolutely not a guilt trip. We cannot sit and place blame on ourselves. We do the best we can, and that will have to be enough.

No family or community is perfect. A person that claims that he has a perfect family protests too much. Ninety-nine percent of all families are dysfunctional and the one percent that claims to not be is in denial. Since the fall of Adam or if one wishes from the beginning of time, human beings have been imperfect. Christians will say we are stained with original sin, other religions will not, but admit we are flawed. Some groups have claimed humankind has been born into a state called Original Blessing, a concept coined from Matthew Fox, a former Catholic priest that denies or downplays original sin. But no matter how we look at ourselves we "ain't perfect," far from it. So what can come out of this book that is useful even without wrapping paper and a ribbon?

We try our best under very adverse conditions. Families try to understand, but usually can't. Why does their son or daughter, husband or wife act the way they do? No one is prepared for mental illness. Each path is a little different. There may be a few predictors that may warn us that clinical depression is coming, but sometimes there aren't. Parents often say "I didn't know there was anything wrong." Outsiders look askance as if to say "How stupid." Yet another time it might be them. Sadly, depression is often a surprise.

But this book has already told us enough about depression and suicide. We know their cultural and causal backgrounds. And we also know about how religions have used their power to dissuade people from committing suicide by threat, cajoling, and even excommunication after death. And none of this has worked. Some religions such as Islam have kept suicides down to just a few, while other cultures have watched them skyrocket, for instance, Japan.

Is there a relationship between culture, cause, and spirituality? There may be. But also there may not be. A Muslim country that forbids suicide may through religion exert control over their people sufficiently that they are afraid to do it for shame or guilt reasons and fear of eternal damnation. They may force their adherents to forego psychological treatment and medication. And still they do not commit suicide. But Muslims as soon as they leave their country of origin commit suicide as much as their neighbors.

Do other religions have the same impact on their followers throughout the ages? It seems not. Suicides seem to be at about the same level as they were in the Middle Ages, population percentage wise.

If a person has a deep spirituality, based on religion or not, this will probably help a person not to commit suicide. If the religious belief is deep, practicing and is not readily accepting of suicide then the person may reconsider the act. But only maybe. Notice the words are deep (ingrained into their souls), practicing (weekly or daily church), and fearful of Hell for committing the act. And even then it is a might not a will. There are no guarantees. Intervention is always a risk. Institutionalization is sometimes only a stop gap effort.

So when does spirituality work? My own observation is when the spirituality involves a "conversion" experience, not to another religion but within oneself. *Metanoia* is a term that means to turn around. To turn around is to convert, to change one's life or lifestyle. Now this is hard if not impossible to do when one is in a state of clinical depression. It must happen before, not after. So someone who has accepted a spirituality before the onset of clinical depression might find that spirituality with medicine and therapy could get them through the "dark night of the soul."

There are no certainties when one is working with the mind and soul. If we look at the stories I have presented in this book, even my own story, there is not really a pattern. People who are religious and spiritual have killed themselves while others have survived. If we look deep enough, we will see a pattern that may escape first glance. I looked. I see only one pattern. A religious or spiritual outlook in life may help a person through the tough times if other help is there as well.

Once again back to my own story. When I was most depressed without medicine or therapy (because I did not know what was wrong with me), I went to church. I partook in the Eucharist. Not just on Sundays but every day of the week I went to Mass. I struggled with myself. I lost hope. I almost despaired. But I didn't. In the darkness of the Night, I saw hope and knew there was meaning to my life.

Meaning is not an easy thing to find once it is lost. But without meaning, why should one stay around? Life rings hollow. We are, St. Paul in First Corinthians, "...a noisy gong, a clanging cymbal." But Paul was not talking about the meaning in life, but love. And what gives us meaning is actually love. And it is in Chapter Thirteen of Corinthians that Paul says in one translation, "Now we see indistinctly, as in a mirror, then we shall see face to face." Mirrors at the time of the Apostle, were not made of glass, rather they were shined metal, frequently bronze. It did not give a clear picture. It was like looking through as glass darkly, where you cannot see the other side because of the darkness. The images are shadows. Or as the blind man who has just had his sight restored to him by Jesus , in the Gospel of Mark, when asked what he sees he says, "I see trees walking." Depression distorts our life.

A last and final story that speaks from my heart. One of the characteristics of bipolar depression is paranoia. One thinks everyone is out to get him. Sometimes, a word or a funny look races through my mind, "what did he or she mean by that?" A friend will say, "You are too sensitive." But clinical depression makes it so. Everything is an innuendo, it means something else. Eventually I am left with a "not trusting anyone" syndrome. That often moves on to the next stage. The world is out to get me. My life is worthless. If my life is worthless then so am I. Therefore my life has no meaning. It is in this stage when thoughts of suicide slip into one's mind. And all this may have come from just a "Good Morning." or a silent stare. Yet none of this was real; rather it is fiction created by an overactive imagination from a dark depression that has left me unable to negotiate the halls of my mind. This happens to me not as much as it used to, but periodically I catch myself doing this step to step approach to self-destruction. Then I reach into my bag of spirituality and pull out something that helps: a meditation exercise or a prayer, a walk in the woods or a visit to the Church.

I found one piece of literature that I memorized, rare for me since I usually hate memorization. It was a poem by W.H. Auden, a British poet, entitled: O Where Are You Going?

"O where are you going?" said reader to rider,

"That valley is fatal when furnaces burn,

Yonder's the midden whose odors will madden,

That gap is the grave where the tall return."

I would recite the words over and over again. I really could not even tell what the words mean to this very day, yet it kept me alive. I would ask myself over and over again, "

"O where are you going?" said reader to rider,

"That valley is fatal when furnaces burn

Yonder's the midden whose odors will madden,

That gap is the grave where the tall return."

Maybe someday, I will have those words tattooed on my arm so when things get bad, I can ask myself the question that is found in its verses "O where are you going?" It can be a poem or a song or a walk in the woods or whatever that allows us to step out of ourselves and be back into the world and be, hopefully, whole again. No matter what it is, it has the ability to jar us out of our mood, and that makes it sacred, holy, even inspired.

Do these things work? Yes. But I must remember to do them or I need someone to remind me to do them. The term I use is often "Beat myself up." While I am musing over what has been done to me, real or unreal, someone will say just that "Don't beat yourself up over this." And I stop and realize that the person is right, I cannot control what other people think or how they respond to me. I cannot control the world around me.

Those who suffer from clinical depression or manic-depression have a mental illness. I think that best sums it up. They suffer from torment of the soul. When we first discussed this book, I called it "Through a Glass Darkly" but Dr. Ang said no, rather Torment of the Soul, and I said, "Oh! Torments of the Soul or The Torment of the Soul." He replied, "No, just Torment of the Soul." So that is the title of the book. The more I say it the more I like it. My soul is tormented when my depression acts up. If only those around me could understand what torment means. It is like when the comic book put a devil among the flames that is sticking a pitch fork into your back. Not to throw off the feeling with a humorous antidote, but it is a constant irritation that seems to never stop. But rather than the devil doing it, life seems to be doing it not lightly, but so it desperately hurts each time. In fact, it is a constant state of pain. Worse than physical pain, it is mental. You want the pain to go away, but it won't. It is torment of--the soul, constant, unending, something that seems will go on forever. The only way to stop is it to end it. I never did, but many do.

Those left behind after someone kills oneself are in pain too. Unable to feel what the person felt, they raise the question 'What could I have done?" The answer is usually nothing. The therapist can only help so much, and is frequently unable to penetrate the self destructiveness or torment of the soul that the suicide is experiencing. The family cannot know what to do because they cannot capture or fathom torment of the soul in any way. The family wants to help, but are powerless. In the end, only a higher power can permeate this state of mind, for any of those involved in the suicide: the person doing it, the therapist, or the family and friends of those who are contemplating such an act. When a soul is tormented, the group just mentioned is powerless.

So we end where we began. Torment of the soul is beyond the healing touch of man. Torment of the Soul, because it is the soul and not just the mind, can only be healed, not cured, only maintained, not erased. We humans can only do so much.

Eventually it is out of our hands. Some people, no matter what they do or we do, cannot become whole again. Recently, a man who survived suicide said, "I have a hole in my soul." At that point, the person, his/her therapist, and family and friends realize that no matter what we do, it will not be enough. At that moment, maybe just before or possibly just after the act of suicide, we have done all that is humanly possible. Once the act has occurred, we know the suicide is finally at peace. What more can we ask than *shalom*, the peace that only God can give? The torment has stopped. The soul is free. No one is guilty. The silence is not that of an empty room, but the silence that Elijah heard on the mountain top after the earthquake and the rumbling from the volcano. With his face turned into the cave, a soft wind kissed his cheek, and then he knew that God was present and all was well.

"But all will be well, and every kind of thing will be well."

- Julian of Norwich

"In my end is my beginning."

- T.S. Eliot

BIBLIOGRAPHY

ARTICLES

Auer, Benedict. "Monastic Asylums," *Human Development*, Vol. 19, Issue 4, (December, 1998), pp. 35-40.

New techniques for Religious Formation," *Human Development*, Vol. 16, Issue 4 (Winter 1995), pp. 12-17.

Baetz, Marilyn, M.D. et al. "Canadian Psychiatric Inpatient Religious Commitment An Association with Mental Health." *The Canadian Journal of Psychiatry*. Vol. 47 [March, 2002]. pp/ 159-166.

Bellah, Robert N. "Religious Evolution," *American Sociological Review*, Vol. 29. No. 3 (June, 1964), pp. 358-374.

Byrd, Jonathan. "Creative Genius or psychotic? A Look at the Strong Positive Correlation Between Creativity and Psychoses." Paper, Rochester Institute of Technology, November 2003.

Coghlan, Cherrie. "Stirring the Dormant Phoenix Reflections on Suicide and Spirituality." Paper delivered at Royal College of Psychiatrists. October 4, 2004.

"'May your God go with you!' Spiritual Themes and Issues in General Psychiatric Setting." 2003.

Culliford, Larry. "Spiritual Care and psychiatric treatment an introduction." *Advances of Psychiatric Treatment.* 2002. Vol. 8, pp. 249-261.

Dervic, Kanita, et al. "Religious Affiliation and Suicide Attempts." *The American Journal of Psychiatry.* December 2004. Vol. 161, pp. 2303-2308.

Fleeter, Patty. "Mental Health Disorders and Spirituality." *Mental Health (MH) Today.* http//www.mental-health-today.com. 2005.

Kauffman, James C. and Baer, John. "I Bask in Dreams of Suicide Mental Illness, Poetry and Women." *Review of General Psychology.* 2002. Vol. 6, No. 3, pp. 271-286.

Mann, John. *Neurobiological Aspects of Suicide.* New York State Office of Mental Health News.

Martin, Graham. "Spirituality and Suicide Prevention." *Auseinetter.* Volume 15 (2), July 2002, pp. 3-4.

Mitchell, Logan and Romans, Sarah. "Spiritual beliefs in bipolar affective disorder their relevance for illness management."

Journal of Affective Disorders. Volume 75, Issue 3 (August, 2003), pp. 247-257.

O'Brien, Sally. "Suicide and Spirituality." Paper delivered at Royal College of Psychiatrists. October 4, 2004. pp. 1-7.

Retterstol,Nils. "Suicide in a Cultural History Perspective, part 1" *The Norwegian Journal of Suicidology*, No. 2. University of Oslo, The Suicide Research and Prevention Unit, 1998.

Rajkowska, Grazyna, *Biological Psychiatry.* 1999.

"Suicide in Cultural History Perspective, part 2," *The Norwegian Journal of Suicidology*, No. 3. University of Oslo, The Suicide Research and Prevention Unit, 2000.

"Suicide in Cultural History Perspective, part 3," *The Norwegian Journal of Suicidology*, No2. University of Oslo, The Suicide Research and Prevention Unit, 1998.

Rolheiser, Ron. " The Notion of Suicide Revisited (Catholic)" Suicide Reference Library. September 24, 2000.

Schreiber, Joseph. "A Sacred Fragility Mental Illness and Spiritual Initial Reflections." *Whosever An Online Magazine for Gay, Lesbian, Bisexual and Transgendered Christians.* 2002.

Sheline, Yvette. Proceedings, National Academy of Science, 1996, Volume 93: 3907-3919.

"Depression Duration but Not Age Predicts Hippocampal Volume Loss in Medically Healthy Women with Recurrent Major Dpression." *Journal of Neuroscience.* 1999, Volume 19 (12): 5034-5043.

Sims, Andrew. "Mysterious Ways: Spirituality and British Psychiatry in the 20th century." Paper delivered Royal College of Psychiatrists (2003).

Stirman,. Whitney, and Pennebaker, James. "Word Use in the poetry of Suicidal and Nonsuicidal Poets." *Psychosomatic Medicine.* Volume 63 (2001), pp. 517-522.

Tacey, David. "Spirituality and the Prevention of Suicide." Paper at 10th Conference of Suicide Prevention National Conference in Australia. June, 2003.

Tamang, Sonam. "Clearing House Thoughts on Depression," Bryn Mawr: Seredipity Press, 2000.

Wasserman, Ira, and Stack, Steven. "The effect of religion on *suicide* An Analysis of cultural context." *Omega Journal of Death and Dying.* 1993. Vol. 27, Issue 4, pp.295-306.

Webb, David. "Suicide Mental Illness or Spiritual Crisis?" Paper at the "Exclusion and Embrace - Conversations about Spirituality and Disability" Melbourne, AustraliaOctober 18-21, 2001.

"The Many Languages of Suicide." Suicide Prevention Australia Conference. Sidney, June, 2002.

Whitney, Edward, M.D. "Mania as Spiritual Emergency." *Psychiatric Services.*Vol. 49, No. 12, December 1998, pp. 1547-1548.

Wilding, Clare, May, Esther, and Muir-Cochrane, Eimear. "Experience of spirituality, mental illness and occupation A life-sustaining phenomenon." *Australian Occupational Therapy Journal.* Volume 52 (March, 2005), pp. 2-9.

Wilding, Clare. "Integrating spirituality, occupation, and mental illness A journey through life of meaningful being and doing." Thesis for MApSc (Occupational Therapy), June 13, 2003.

Books

Auer, Benedict, O.S.B. *Soulpoeting Healing through Poetry.* London St. Paul's Publications, 2000.

Casey, Nell (Editor). *Unholy Ghost Writers on Depression.* New York Perennial, 2001.

Capuzzi, Dave. *Preventing adolescent suicide.* Accelerated Development, 1988.

Doka, Kenneth J. with John D. Morgan. *Death and Spirituality.* Amityville, N.Y.: Baywood Pub. Co., 1993.

Durkheim, Emile. *Suicide A Study in Sociology.* Translated by John A. Spaulding and George Simpson. Glencoe, IL. Free Press. 1951.

Egremont, Max. *Siegfried Sassoon A Life*. New York Ferrar, Straus & Giroux, 2005.

Ferrucci, Piero. *What We May Be The Vision and Techniques of Pscyhosynthesis*. London Thorsons, 1982.

Francis, Dorothy Brenner. *Suicide a preventable tragedy*. New York Lodestar Books,1989.

Goodwin, Frederick K, and Jamison, Kay R. *Manic-Depressive Illness*. Oxford University Press, 1990.

(Update coming).

Goldsmith, S.K. et al. *Reducing Suicide A national imperative*. Committee on Pathophysiology and Prevention of Aadolescent Suicide, Board of Neuroscience and Behavioral Health, Institute of Medicine. Washington, D.C. National Academies Press, 2002.

Grollman, Earl A. *Suicide Presvention, Intervention, Post-intervention*. Boston Beacon Press, 1988.

Jamison, Kay Redfield. *An Unquiet Mind A Memoir of Moods and Madness*. New York Vintage Books, 1995.

Night Falls Fast Understanding Suicide.New York Vintage Books, 1999.

Touched by Fire Manic-Depressive Illness and the Artistic Temperment. New York Vintage Books, *Exuberance The Passion for Life.* New York Vintage Books, 2004.

Kenyon, Jane. *Collected Poems.* Minneapolis Graywolf, 2005.

Klein, Donald F. and Wernder, Paul H. *Understanding Depression A Complete Guide to its Diagnosis and Treatment.* New York Oxford University Press, 1993.

Koterski, Joseph (editor). *Life and Learning VIII Proceedings of the University Faculty for Life Conference June 1998 at the University of Toronto.* Washington, D.C. University Faculty for Life, 1999.

Kramer, Peter. *Against Depression* New York Penguin Books, 2005.

Kuklin, Susan. *After a suicide young people speak up.* New York Putnam, 1994.

Matthew, Iain. *The Impact of God: Soundings from St. John of the Cross.* London Hodder and Stoughton, 1995.

Maris, Ronald W. (editor). *Assessment and Prediction of Suicide.* New York Guildford Press, 1992.

Minois, Georges. *A History of Suicide: Voluntary Death in Western Culture.* Johns Hopkins Univerisity, 1999.

Mondimore, Francis Mark. *Bipolar A Guide for Patients and Families.* Baltimore The John Hopkins University Press, 1999.

Murphy, James. *Coping With Teen Suicide*. New York Rosen Press, 1999.

Nelson, John E. and Nelson, Andrea (Editors). *Sacred Sorrows Embracing and Transforming Depression*. New York Jeremy P. Tarcher/Putnam, 1996.

Plath, Sylvia. *The Bell Jar*. New York Bantam Books, 1971, 1988.

Quinn, Brian P. *The Depression Sourcebook*. Second Edition. Lakewood, IL Lowell House, 2000.

Quinnett, Paul G. *Suicide The Forever Decision For those thinking about suicide and for those who know, love, or counsel them*. New York Continuum, 1992.

Retterstol, Nils. *Suicide: A European Perspective*. Cambridge: Cambridge University Press, 1994.

Roethke, Theodore. *The Collected Poems*. New York Anchor Press, 1975.

Rosenberg, Jay F. *Thinking Clearly About Death*. Indianapolis Hackett Pub. Co, 1998.

Sexton, Anne. *The Complete Poems*. New York Houghton Mifflin Company, 1981.

Shneidman, Edwin S. *Comprehending Suicide landmarks in 20th century suicidology*. Washington, D.C. American Psychological Association, 2001.

Sinetar, Marsha. *Don't Call Me Old - I'm Just Awakening Spiritual Encouragement for Later Life.* New York Paulist Press, 2002.

Spiritual Intelligence What we can learn from the early awakening of a Child. Maryknoll Orbis Books, 2000.

A Way Without Words A Guide for Spiritually Emerging Adults. New York Paulist Press, 1992.

Ordinary People as Monks and Mystics Lifestyles for Self-discovery. New York Paulist Press, 1986.

Solomon, Andrew. *The Noonday Demon: An Atlas of Depression.* New York Scribner, 2001.

Steinfels, Margaret Mary O'Brien (editor). *American Catholics, American Culture Tradition and Resistence.* Ladham, MD Rowman and littlefield, 2004.

Tacey, David. *Spiritual Perspectives on Suicidal Impulses in Young Adults.* Colorado Springs Colorado School of Psychology Press, 2005.

Wallace, Samuel. *After Suicide.* New York Wiley, 1973.

Walsh, Froma and McGoldrick, Monica (ed). *Living Beyond Loss: Death in the Family.* New York: WW Norton, 2004.

INTERVIEWS, E-MAILS, AND LETTERS

E-mails and Materials on Mark Samco by his father, Rick Samco and his professor at Dartmouth College, Dr. Peter U. Tse.

Obituary and E-mail provided by Archabbot Justin Duvall, O.S.B., of St. Meinrad Archabbey, IN

Lisa Watkins from a paper entitled "Spirituality and Mental Illness" done a Course entitled The Spiritual Quest at St. Martin's University in Lacey, WA

Personal Experiences and Reminiscences of Father Benedict Auer, O.S.B.